Video Game Addiction 101

Video Game Addiction 101

a primer on Internet Gaming Disorder

Andrew Walsh

and

Frank L. Greenagel II

Wooden Nail Press
Phillipsburg, New Jersey

Contents

Preface 6

Introduction 10

History of Gaming 14

Gaming in the United States 27

Gaming in Asia 40

Psychology of Game Design 65

Recognizing Addiction 80

A Recovery Story 92

Recommendations 115

Moving Forward 122

Appendices

Addiction Professional 138

Current Analysis 141

Glossary 146

Bibliography 154

Index 159

Screening Checklist 166

Preface

The World Health Organization (WHO) stated that video game addiction was a problem in June of 2018 (the official term they use is *Internet Gaming Disorder*). The WHO's announcement was big news, and it was reported in major articles in the *New York Times* and the *Washington Post*. We read the stories and did some digging. We talked to school social workers and parents. We met with students from the Rutgers University Recovery House. By the end of June, we were beginning to realize that it was a far bigger problem than most counseling and other health-care professionals could conceive.

Andrew and I sat down on my porch, and over a cup of tea and a strong cigar we mapped out the purpose of the book and the content of each individual chapter. He did all the research and reference work and wrote the first draft of his chapters. I served as the front-line editor and my father cleaned up what I missed. We are all grateful for our early readers and their feedback. We must make a particular show of thanks to Matt from the Rutgers Recovery House who shared his story and insights—they appear near the end of this book.

Internet gaming disorder (I actually prefer the term *video game addiction*) is a tricky topic. The problem is real and growing every year, but there are very few treatment programs in the United States that are addressing it. Most of them are just guessing on how to treat it. We hope that this book will spur a conversation and influence a variety of parents, educators, researchers, policy makers and clinicians to improve the prevention and treatment of video game addiction.

I hope that you will read this book from beginning to end. We begin with the history of video games (they started in the United

States) and the development of the industry. We then move on to examine four Asian countries, whose problems are worse but solutions further along. The chapter on the business of gaming provides shocking economic numbers (originally a chapter, it's been moved to the appendix as it's supplemental and not essential). It is because of the staggering amount of money and geometric growth that we believe that this problem is only going to get far worse over the next few years. We wrote, edited, threw out, rewrote and edited the psychology and recognizing addiction chapters over the last year. There is a story about a young man who has been in recovery for over three years. He also answered a number of my questions in an interview and then in written form. In one of the final chapters, Andrew provides some basic recommendations for parents, educators, researchers, policy makers and clinicians. My chapter titled "Moving Forward" contains some random thoughts that sprang out of our work this last year, a summary of our major points, and a quick plan for families and clinicians.

We ended up working on this book for over a year (I had planned on getting it out by Dec 31, 2018 but both research and life got in the way). The delay allowed us to include what we learned by treating several people at our Florham Park office as well as presenting to groups large and small around New Jersey for the Rutgers Center of Alcohol Studies, the National Association of Social Workers (NASW-NJ), Advanced Counselor Training, and the New Jersey Family and Addiction Institute (our program in Florham Park). We are really grateful to the questions and feedback we received while teaching and counseling. They have made our knowledge, work and this book far better.

We are hoping to conduct a few studies (with university partnerships) over the next two years as well as collect a few more case narratives. We expect to release *Video Game Addiction 201* once that aforementioned work is complete.

If you are a parent in distress, you might want to read just the Introduction, a story of addiction and recovery, and the Recommendations. If you are a clinician pressed for time, you probably will skip the history and business chapters and focus on the psychology, recognizing, recommendations and moving forward. If you are a policy maker, you must read the chapters on Asia and the business of gaming. Hopefully you will read them all though.

Frank L. Greenagel II

September 1, 2019
Piscataway, NJ

Introduction

In the fall of 2011, a staff psychologist brought a student into my office. The psychologist looked a bit stressed. She introduced us to each other. I learned that he was a 27 year old international student from Korea who had come to the counseling center at the behest of his parents. The psychologist looked and me and said, "This is the kind of case that we think you might be the best fit for."

Some background: I specialize in substance misuse treatment and recovery support services. I had been working at Rutgers for a little over two years. Students were often referred to me by psychologists, psychiatrists, student affairs, or the Dean's office, but that was usually by phone or email and with several days or weeks' notice. In what would be a five year career at the Rutgers New Brunswick and Newark Counseling Centers, I only had another counseling professional bring a student to my office on the same day about 10 times. Those were all screaming cases that consisted of either beyond the pale addiction, a veteran with complex trauma, or spectacular drug distribution charges. I enjoyed my reputation for being able to deal with the heavy and brutal cases that frustrated, shocked or frightened other counselors. I was definitely intrigued.

When we were alone, I offered the student some water. He turned it down. He sat in a chair opposite me and kept his bag on his lap. He had a furtive expression and he avoided making eye contact. I told him about confidentiality laws and how his conversation with me was completely protected, with five exceptions which I clearly but quickly explained. I told him that I wouldn't tell his parents or professors or anyone else in his life anything unless he gave me a signed release to do so. I informed him that I specialized in addiction and that I was curious about his story.

He decided to take the bottle of water and then asked me what I know about video games. Instead of answering his question and then slowly getting to know him, I took a shot and asked, "Do you play *World of Warcraft?*"

His eyes lit up. "Yes."

"Is that why you are here?"

"Yes."
He was making direct eye contact with me now.

"What level are you?"

"Eighty."

"How many characters do you have?"

He smiled. "Seven."

"What are their levels?"

He smiled again. "Eighty." I could tell he appreciated my knowledge (which was very basic and solely based on my interactions with students from the Rutgers Recovery House).

"Has playing *World of Warcraft* affected your grades?"

"Yes. Yes. Yes."

"Before I can help you, I need to learn more."

Over the next hour, he shared all of the humiliating (his word, not mine) details. This was his 19th semester at Rutgers. He had enough credits to be considered a second semester junior. He had failed more classes than he had passed, and he attributed all of his problems to his gaming addiction.[1] There was one period where he never left his off-campus apartment for a period of six weeks, and that there were multiple other times where he stayed in his apartment for three straight weeks. He reported that he had some health problems due to lack of eating, but that he had recently seen a doctor and had put on eight pounds. The doctor sent a report to his mother and had suggested counseling. The young man had resisted but his parents had threatened to cut him off if he didn't go. He told me that he needed a letter from me that he had come. I told him I needed a signed record release for that. He was sharp. He said he'd only grant me the release for the purpose of writing the letter.

When I asked him about his friends, he told me about his online playing partners. "I mean your friends in the real world."

He winced at the "real" comment. I made a note to come up with a better term next time. "No. All my friends are from the game."

He told me about how he had tried to reduce or quit playing *World of Warcraft* (WoW) several times. He had taken the game off his computer. And then put it back on. Over and over. He had signed up for some program that made it impossible for him to put WoW back on. Then he cracked open his computer and took it apart until he was able to put WoW back on. One time, he signed up for some program that put a virtual lock on WoW and then gave the passcode to a classmate. He texted, called, and emailed the young man for the passcode. To his classmate's credit, he refused to give it to him and told him that he

---

1 Rutgers had clearly failed this young man. I can think of no scenario that is acceptable for the school to continue to take his money (a huge sum for international students) year after year and not address all of the failing grades. There should have been meetings with the Dean and the health center and, of course, eventually the counseling center. The worst part of this footnote to consider is that I'm sure this situation has been repeated hundreds, if not thousands, of times on campuses across the United States.

should study. Enraged, my client showed up at his apartment and banged on the door until he got the passcode.

I wrote his parents that he had come to see me and that I was very concerned about his gaming addiction and that I wanted him to return. I showed it to him. He begrudgingly took it. I tried to get him to schedule a future appointment, but he refused. He said that he only had to come to one appointment in order not to be cut off financially.[2]

I never saw him again.

Since then, I've treated a few dozen clients (mostly young males) for gaming addiction. Many of them also have or had co-occurring substance misuse disorders. The aforementioned story was the most extreme case. I don't usually like talking about the most extreme examples of cases, but this story works very well to open up a book on video game addiction. Despite the extreme playing and the long-standing problems that it caused, the young man experienced consequences that are quite common: malnutrition, weight loss, social isolation, academic difficulties, and family conflict.

---

2 Note to family members. Be very careful and very clear about whatever deals you make.

A History of Gaming

Modern gaming traces its roots back to the 1940 World's Fair in New York. At the Fair Dr. Edward Uhler Condon presented *Nimatron*, the first computer game. Nimatron pitted players against a computer in a game focused on turning off lights. The game was very popular and an estimated 100,000 people played it during the Fair.

While today one might envision a computer game designer as a twenty-something geek with a ratty T-shirt and an unkempt appearance, that was far from the case in 1940. Condon was a prominent American nuclear physicist who made significant contributions to the development of radar and nuclear weapons.

As the technology to create games did not exist, it took a world renowned nuclear physicist to create it. After the Fair there were limited advancements in gaming over the next three decades; that changed in 1967 with Ralph Baer. Baer's family fled to the United States when he was teenager prior to the start of World War II to escape antisemitism persecution. Upon arriving in the U.S., Baer soon developed an interest in electronics and went on to become an inventor who filed over 150 patents during the course of his life.

While only 9% of households had televisions in 1950, that number grew to over 90% by 1960. Having witnessed the growth of television, one idea in particular intrigued Baer: combining television screens with playing games. Baer's employer, Sanders Associates (a defense contractor), gave him a small budget to work on his idea. It took him several attempts but he was eventually successful. Baer's plans called for a wood veneer for the console. He exhausted the budget provided to him. Ever creative, he wrapped the console in brown masking tape as a substitute for wood to save costs. This led to his prototype to being referred to as "the brown box." In 1971, Baer licensed his prototype to Magnavox and it was renamed *Magnavox Odyssey*. Magnavox Odyssey went on to become the first game console and over 340,000 units were sold. For his work as the pioneer in the gaming industry, Ralph Baer is called "the Father of Video Games."

Coming on the heels of the release of the *Odyssey* was the release of an arcade game called *Pong*. *Pong* laid the foundation for video game arcades. *Pong* was the brainchild of Nolan Bushnell and Ted Dabney. Bushnell and Dabney started working together in 1969 when they formed a company called Syzygy and created a coin-operated machine game called *Computer Space*.

While their game was a commercial failure, they applied the lessons they learned from this experience in the formation of their next company, which was called Atari. The first major release for Atari was *Pong* in a coin-operated form in 1972. Having successfully created *Pong*, Bushnell and Dabney found they didn't have a significant budget for marketing. Seeking to get feedback, they placed the *Pong* prototype arcade game in their local tavern. Approximately one week later, they received a call from the bar's owner saying the game was having technical problems. Terrified that something was wrong with their prototype, they immediately had the machine inspected. They learned that the coin mechanism was overflowing with quarters because the game had been played so much. In that instant, Bushnell and Dabney realized they had a hit. *Pong* helped initiate what would come to known as the golden age of arcades (which lasted until the early 1980s).

The creation of video game consoles and arcades served as the foundation of the video game industry. The next significant stride forward was the creation of multiplayer gaming. While multiplayer options are nearly infinite today, their beginnings were much more limited in their capabilities. Responding to customer demands, restaurants in the 1970s started to add arcade games. Initially, customers spent hours playing games to try and beat the high score. Players would compete against the game and then compare high scores with their friends. Soon, gaming industry leaders realized that direct competition against other players would be the next step forward. Consumers eagerly anticipated the opportunity to compete directly against their friends. In 1973, they got their wish.

Plato Network System (Plato Logic for Automatic Teaching Operation) was a computer network created by the University of Illinois for teaching purposes in 1961. In 1973, John Daleske, then a student at Iowa State University, created a game he called *Empire* for a class project. Players got to compete directly against each other with up to 30 players playing st once. Empire went on to become the first multiplayer game and was reportedly to have been played for over 3 million hours by 1980.

In 1977 Atari released their second game console which they named the *Atari 2600*. This model had an external read only memory (ROM) slot which allowed users to plug in different game cartridges. ROM was important in video game design because it allowed for games not to take up the limited memory space on game consoles. The inclusion of the external ROM slot allowed users more gaming options. Prior to this, users could only select from one of the ten games that were included in the console.

While Ralph Baer's first console was a novelty item, the Atari 2600 officially initiated the console market. This new ability to play additional games spurred a new wave of video game creation.

The game market and the console market were saturated in North America at the start of the 1980s. Players could select from a variety of consoles that allowed users to select which games they wanted to play. To meet this new demand for options, video game design companies dramatically increased their production of games. These companies sacrificed quality for quantity. In 1983, the gaming market generated approximately $3.2 billion in North America. By 1985, revenue plummeted to $100 million, a 97% decrease. The North American video game industry was declared dead.

Except it wasn't.

For workers in the North American video game industry, 1985 most likely started with a flurry of updating resumes and looking for more stable employment as the industry collapsed. By the end of the year, the North American market was back in business due to the furious competition between two Japanese companies who desperately fought to own the North American market. In the process of trying to destroy each other, these companies saved the North American market. Thus the console wars between Nintendo Entertainment Systems (NES) and Sega began.

Nintendo quickly struck the first blow of this battle by being first to market in the U.S. Their console was released in 1985 and was called the Nintendo Entertainment System. Nintendo's NES console quickly took the number one spot in the market due to its superior graphics, sounds, colors, and gameplay. Having studied the 1983 crash, Nintendo realized that over-hyped and poor quality video games contributed significantly to the downturn. Several companies had gone out of business. To avoid a similar fate, Nintendo focused on the quality of the video games that they produced. Nintendo developed many of the games in-house and produced fan favorites such as *Super Mario Bros.*, *Metroid*, and *The Legend of Zelda*.

While Nintendo initially enjoyed little competition, Sega entered into the North American market in 1986 with the release of their console the Sega Master System. The console only achieved moderate success and did little to compete against Nintendo's NES. In 1989 Sega released a new console called Sega Genesis. Initially sales for the Sega Genesis were below expectations. Facing the threat of losing a market share in North America, Sega hired Tom Kalinske, an industry outsider, to overhaul their North American division. One of the main contributors to the competitive advantages Nintendo had over Sega was the quality of its games which it bundled with purchases of the game console.

At the time Sega had copied the process and was including the game *Altered Beast* with the purchase of the Genesis. While the Genesis was a great console, players thought *Altered Beast* was a terrible game. Tom Kalinske realized that the survival of Sega in North America hinged on significant improvements in game offerings. After a company-wide competition for a new video game character, Sega released *Sonic the Hedgehog*, which went on to become one of the most popular games of all time. With Sega's release of the *Hedgehog*, the fierce battle took off.

Just as Sega was getting their legs under themselves in the North American market, Nintendo pivoted and expanded into a new market: handheld mobile game consoles. They exploded into this market with the release of Game Boy in 1989. The importance of the Game Boy will be discussed later.

As the competition heated up between Nintendo and Sega, each company attempted to one up the other. Hayao Nakayama was the president of the Japanese branch of Sega and overall authority for Sega in North America. As a child Nakayama had grown up witnessing the Coca-Cola and Pepsi battle in the early 1980s. When approached with the idea of having Sega do a negative ad campaign against Nintendo, Nakayama did not hesitate to give his approval. Shortly thereafter the Sega campaign titled "Genesis does what Nintendo can't" was launched and the feud went into hyper drive.

As a result of being first to market, Nintendo controlled 90% of the U.S. video game market by 1990. However, due to the success of its "Genesis does what Nintendo can't" and its superior graphics, Sega overtook Nintendo as the market leader in the U.S in 1992.

While this success in the North American market was great for Sega North America, it laid the seeds for its future destruction. The success of Sega in the U.S. far outpaced the success of Sega in Japan. For years Sega Japan executives heard how the North American branch was performing so much better than the Japanese branch. Eventually the Sega Japan executives could not tolerate it anymore and actively started to undermine Sega North

America. This jealously would eventually significantly weaken Sega in North America.

Silicon Graphics was a computer manufacturer that produced both hardware and software and had extensive capabilities in 3D imaging. Founded in 1981, Silicon Graphics enjoyed enormous success due their 3D graphical capabilities and products. By 1996 Silicon Graphics quickly lost its market share and struggled financially. Silicon Graphics CEO Ed McCracken had been paying attention to the growing video game market and approached Sega North America about a partnership. Sega North America was excited. The executives from Sega Japan reviewed the potential partnership with Silicon Graphics and saw an opportunity to undermine their fellow executives who had been beating them for years. The Sega Japan executives killed the deal between Sega and Silicon Graphics.

Forced to find another company to partner with, Silicon Graphics approached Nintendo to see if they were interested in the new computer chip that they had developed for a next generation game console. Nintendo quickly realized the potential of the new computer chip and agreed to a partnership. Using the new chip Nintendo launched Nintendo 64 in 1996 to great success in North America. Failing to make a deal with Silicon Graphics and then witnessing Silicon Graphics make a deal with their direct competitor marked the start of the demise for Sega.

Nintendo was not immune to serious blunders. In 1995, Nintendo and Sega were competing for second place in the game console market. While Sega's blunder in passing on Silicon Graphics' chip allowed Nintendo to win second place, Nintendo's own blunder prevented it from owning the largest market share. In 1988, Nintendo and Sony were working on a secret joint-venture to create a CD-ROM for Nintendo. Nintendo publicly denied the existence of a partnership with Sony as late as 1991. In June of 1992, the executive team of Sony met to determine if they would move forward with the release of their own game console. During the meeting, Sony President Norio Ohga was reminded by one of his deputies of the public humiliation he experienced from Nintendo. Infuriated, President Ohga decided to move forward with Sony releasing its own game console. In 1994 Sony released the *Playstation*, and eventually went on to sell over 120 million consoles.

The personal computer

In the late 1970s and early 1980s, the computer industry was making significant strides in making personal computers more accessible to the general public. In 1972, Hewlett-Packard created a small business computer which retailed for $95,000. Adjusted for inflation this equates to over half a million dollars today. Apple released the Apple I in 1976 and the Apple II in 1977 for $667 and $1298 respectively. By the 1980s the Commodore Vic-20, with a price of $299, became the first personal computer to sell over one million units.

In the early 1980s, the United States entered into a recession. Inflation, which had been high in the 1970s, skyrocketed to a high of 13.5% in 1980, which was the highest since the Great Depression. Unemployment hit 10.8% in 1982. Households became more selective in their purchases.

While the video game and console market crash in 1983 is predominately attributed to oversupply and poor quality of video games and consoles, the recession also contributed. With the standard household experiencing financial constraints, purchases became highly scrutinized. People elected to purchase a computer, which had become affordable at this time instead of a game console, because computers could also be used for educational purposes. At the time that home computer sales were increasing, BASIC was the most common computer coding language. BASIC was high-level enough to do actual programming while simultaneously being small enough to fit on the computers. During the late 1970s and early 1980s, computer magazines started to publish the source code for various video games. These allowed

computer owners to simply type in the code from the magazine
and then play them. A whole generation of computer game cod-
ers was born and would go on to shape the gaming industry.

From 1983 to 1988, personal computer gaming was able to
flourish unhindered as the game console market continued to
flounder. However, with the release of the Nintendo game console in 1985, game consoles started to overtake computer games
in popularity. By 1993, the game console market generated $5.9
billion in revenue compared to $430 million in the computer-
games market. Computer-games made significant contributions
to the shaping of the gaming field overall during this period. The
age of the PC just had not fully arrived.

Internet based consoles

B y the end of the century, Sony controlled the North American console market followed by Nintendo, Sega, and Atari.
The next major advancement in the gaming industry came from
combining game consoles with the internet. Nintendo quickly
produced *Satellaview* in 1995. Satellaview was a satellite mo-
dem that subscribers could download video games and content
directly to their console from the satellite. Satellaview was never
a commercial success. It was discontinued in 2000 but it set the
stage for modern day consoles with internet capabilities.

Nintendo, Sega, and Atari made repeated attempts to capture
the online console industry in the late 1990s but continually
failed. In 2000, Sega released a new generation game console
called *Dreamcast*. The Sega Dreamcast was built with expensive
components that allowed users to access the internet directly.
Including these components dramatically increased the cost of
the Sega Dreamcast. However broadband internet access was not
as widespread as Sega executives had anticipated. At that time
using the internet was quite expensive and still relied on dial-up.
The Sega Dreamcast ended up competing with the Sony PlaySta-

tion2 which cost significantly less. This forced Sega to sell the Dreamcast at a substantial loss which ensured the financial failure of the Dreamcast.

Following the Dreamcast, Sega divested from the console business completely. In less than two decades Sega, helped save the North American gaming market, ascended to the top position, and nearly went bankrupt. Sega helped drive the gaming industry forward with both its successes and failures. The failure of the Dreamcast provided the foundation on which the modern game console market is currently built. Eventually Sony, Microsoft, and Nintendo would create viable gaming systems.

The Modern Age of Gaming

Milestones in gaming advancements can be marked by the release of important games and consoles. The first game to alter the landscape of modern gaming was developed by id Software. They released the computer game *Doom* in 1993. *Doom* was a first person shooter game in which a space marine fights demons from hell. The game was tremendously violent and involved lots of gore. To keep marketing and overhead costs low, id Software released *Doom* via shareware. The company allowed users to download the game for free and encouraged them to share the game with friends. This strategy proved to be effective as over one million people elected to purchase the registered version of *Doom* after playing it for free. Many mistakenly believe that *Doom* was the first game to involve "deathmatches." A death-match is a multiplayer option in which players fight each other until only one player is left alive. The distinction for the first game to offer deathmatches actually belongs to the computer game *Maze War*. However, the gore in *Doom* and advancements in internet capability made *Doom* deathmatches very popular. It was so popular that within two years of its release an estimated twenty million people played the game. Employees playing *Doom* during work decreased productivity so much that corporations such as Intel and universities such as Carnegie Melon had to develop policies that strictly prohibited playing *Doom* during business hours.

Blizzard Entertainment released the computer game *StarCraft* in 1998. *StarCraft* was set in the future and focused on three alien races trying to force the other two to assimilate. It proved to be a commercial success; 1.5 million copies were sold in 1998 and 9.5 million copies by 2008. Over 4.5 million copies of *StarCraft* were sold in South Korea alone. Eventually *StarCraft* became the basis for the creation of the professional gaming industry in South Korea, and eventually the world. *StarCraft* is often critically acclaimed as being the best real-time strategy game ever made.

The next major advancement in the gaming industry came in 2001 when Microsoft became the first American company to step back into the arena of game console production with the release of *Xbox*. Microsoft initially sold Xbox at a loss to gain a market share in the North American market. While the console was praised for its capabilities, Xbox's popularity exploded when a subsidiary of Microsoft created the game *Halo* specifically for Xbox. *Halo* is set in the future and pits genetically engineered humans against an alien race attempting to destroy Earth. Over 50% of people who purchased Xbox simultaneously purchased *Halo*, resulting in *Halo* becoming one of the most profitable video games of all time. The *Halo* franchise is currently estimated to be worth in excess of $5 billion. In 2018 the Dallas Cowboys franchise was valued at $4 billion, making it the most valuable professional sports franchise in the world. *Halo* is more valuable than any professional sports team in the world.

Activision released *Call of Duty* for Microsoft Windows in 2003. It was a tremendously popular PC game. *Call of Duty* was adapted for consoles and began sales in 2008. Activision has continued to release a new installment of the *Call of Duty* franchise on a yearly basis since 2008. For comparative purposes, Marvel has released 20 movies since 2008 which have generated approximately $17 billion in box office sales worldwide. Activision has released 10 new installments in the *Call of Duty* franchise since 2008 and has grossed over $11 billion in revenue.

Blizzard Entertainment again impacted the gaming community with their fourth installment of the Warcraft fantasy universe which was called *World of Warcraft* (WOW). WOW is a massive multiplayer online role playing game (MMORPG) in which players select an avatar to fight others and go on quests. WOW won the award for "Most Addictive Game of the Year" in 2005. In 2010, WOW had over 12 million subscribers who paid a monthly subscription fee of $15. At its peak WOW was generating $180 million per month in subscription fees and held 62% of the MMORPG subscription market.

The next dominant game was *League of Legends*, which was developed by Riot Games and released in 2009. *League of Legends* quickly became the most popular multiplayer online battle arena (MOBA) of all time. At its peak, *League of Legends* had 27 million daily users and over 60 million monthly users.

PC games initially dominated the start of the modern gaming age, but with the release of smartphones in 2007, the gaming industry underwent another revolution. According to the United Nations, more people have cell phones (6 billion) than have toilets (4.5 billion). An estimated 56% of people in the United States alone report using their mobile devices to play video games every month.

Leading the wave on cell phone games, Rovio Mobile created a game for cellphones called *Angry Birds* in 2009. In the game, players use a slingshot to defend bird eggs from pigs. *Angry Birds* was originally offered as a free download, and eventually over 11 million people downloaded the free version. However, the game was so popular that over 7 million consumers purchased the full-featured paid version which cost $0.99 for smartphones and $2.99 for IPads. On average only 2% of users who download an app make purchases. This means that *Angry Birds* had one of the highest conversion rates of all time.

The release of two more mobile device games in 2012 helped solidify mobile gaming ahead of console gaming revenue. *Candy Crush* was released by developer King and was available free of charge to download. Players seek to match pieces of candy to get three or more of the same color in a row. The game proved to be very popular and by 2014 had over 245 million active users. While the game was free to download, users were able to make in-game purchases including extra lives or extra moves. Purchases in 2014 alone were $1.3 billion. *Candy Crush* went on to become the most downloaded game from the App Store of all time with over 2.73 billion downloads since its creation. Today players swipe over 71,000 miles per day playing *Candy Crush*.

The other game was Supercell's *Clash of Clans*. It is a fantasy game in which the player is the chief of a village who builds his town with plunder stolen from other towns. The game quickly became one of the most downloaded games from the App Store. By 2015, *Clash of Clans* was generating $1.5 million per day in revenue though the App Store and Google Play. *Clash of Clans* has been credited with creating the new era of using mobile devices for single player gaming.

Although mobile gaming now generates more revenue than console gaming, it would be a mistake to assume that video game consoles have fallen by the wayside. In 2018, game developers Epic Games and People Can Fly released *Fortnite*. *Fortnite* can be played on smartphones or consoles. As of the summer of 2018, 125 million people play *Fortnite*. Revenue for *Fortnite* has continued to grow on a monthly basis with April 2018 generating approximately $300 million.

This chapter was meant to be a brief history lesson on the gaming industry overall. This is meant to provide background information as you move through the rest of the book. The gaming industry history has shown tremendous evolution over its short existence. Approximately 50 years ago the first game console was released. It was initially wrapped in brown masking tape because wood was too expensive. Today game franchises are worth more than professional sport franchises. The gaming industry history illustrates rapid growth and development. There is no reason to believe the furious rate of growth and development will stop in the gaming industry.

Gaming in the United States

The United States created the video game industry when
Edward Condon laid the groundwork with *Nimatron* at the
World's Fair in 1940. The 1970s ushered in the age of game
consoles with the release of the *Odyssey*. The popularity of
video games in the U.S. increased dramatically from the 1970s
to the early 1980s. In response to increased demand, U.S. game
producers flooded the market with subpar video games, which
caused the market to collapse. During the mid-1980s crash,
video game industry revenue in North America plummeted 97%.
The industry in the U.S. eventually did recover a few years later,
spurred by competition between Sega and Nintendo along with
the release of popular games such as *Doom*. Prompted by the
console releases of Sony PlayStation and Microsoft Xbox, the
gaming industry experienced rapid growth at the dawn of the new
century. The U.S. industry went from near death in 1985 to being
the second largest video game market in the world in 2017.

In a 2018 survey, 66% of Americans over the age of 13 identified themselves as *gamers*. In 2016, the gaming industry generated three times as much revenue as the film industry box office
sales and four times as much revenue as the music industry.
Watching others play video games, whether in-person or on television, is called electronic sports, or eSports for short. eSports was
projected to generate $345 million in revenue in North America
in 2018 and expected to double by 2021. A 2017 survey by the
University of Massachusetts found that three-quarters of 14-21
year olds watched others play video games online at least once
in the past 12 months. The survey also found that 38% identified
as being fans of eSports and competitive gaming. Comparatively
the survey also found that 40% of 14-21 year olds are fans of the

NFL. eSports and competitive gaming is as popular as the NFL in this age group.

While the popularity of eSports in the U.S. lags behind the popularity of eSports in Asian countries, it is becoming more widespread and accepted. In 2014, Robert Morris University became the first to have an eSports collegiate team.

Approximately one hundred colleges and universities in the U.S. now field varsity level eSports teams and typically provide athletic scholarships, housing, and training gear for team members. The table below shows the prize money for major eSports events as well as traditional sporting events.

DOTA stands for *Defense of the Ancients* and is a massive online battle arena game in which teams fight each other to the death. The 2018 DOTA 2 international world championship had a prize purse of $25.5 million dollars. That is 65% more than the Daytona 500, which features the best racers in the world, and more than double the purse for the U.S. Open, which is comprised of the best golfers in the world. LoL stands for *League of Legends*, which is also a massive online battle arena game in which teams fight to destroy the base of opposing teams. Approximately 43 million people watched the LoL championship in 2017.

Further illustrating the growing popularity of eSports in the U.S., the National Basketball Association partnered with Take-Two Interactive to form the NBA 2K League in 2017. In its inaugural season, there were 17 teams that were affiliated with actual NBA teams. NBA commissioner Adam Silver said, "From the NBA's standpoint, this is our fourth league." Players earn between $32,000 to $35,000 over six months and are provided housing, meals, and training facilities. Games are broadcast on television and streamed on YouTube and Twitch.

Gamers in the U.S.

Let us identify the gamers. I know you may read that and won-der, "Why is he going to take time to describe gamers? After all I already know what they are like." The common stereotype of gamers is typically some combination of being male, overweight, pale from lack of sun, nerdy, and socially awkward. Researchers conducted surveys and determined that the stereotypes of gamers involve several themes: unattractive, unpopular, socially incom-petent, and obsession with gaming. In reality the typical gamer in the U.S. does not resemble this stereotype.

Gender

One common belief is that almost all gamers are men. Few think of women living in their parents' basement playing video games. Studies estimate that up to 45% of game players are female. Trends regarding gender and video game playing are il-lustrated in the graph below. Popularity of gaming among women peaked in 2014 at 48% and declined to 45% in 2018. Gaming among females increased significantly from 2006 when females represented 38% of gamers. Females are almost as likely as males to play games. Increases in mobile gaming has been cited as the cause of increases in gaming among women.[1]

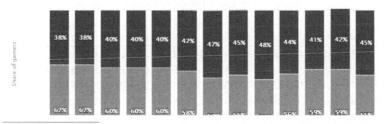

1 https://www.washingtonpost.com/news/morning-mix/wp/2014/08/22/ adult-women-gamers-outnumber-teenage-boys/?noredirect=on&utm_ term=.c24676978304

Age

The typical notion is that gamers are usually young-adults. The graph on the next page shows the age breakdown of video game players in the U.S. as of 2018. The average gamer is actually between 18 and 35 years old. This is older than the stereotype. An estimated 57% of gamers are younger than 36 years old. What is very surprising is that 43% of gamers are 36 years old or older, including 23% who are over the age of 50. Just 29% of gamers are technically young adults.

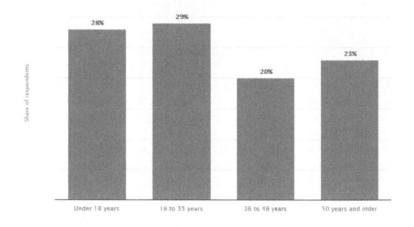

Uneducated

The stereotypical gamer lacks education and prefers to play video games rather than go to school. Studies have suggested this stereotype may be false. Comparing gamers to non-gamers, gamers are more likely to be college-educated with 43% of gamers being college-educated compared to 36% of non-gamers. Additionally, gamers' parents are more likely to be college-educated (52%) than the parents of non-gamers (37%).

Unemployed

We have established that gaming is not gender-specific, is played by all ages, and has many players who are educated. You might think, "There is no way that these people are employed. How would they work and play their little games?" It turns out that gamers have higher rates of full-time employment (42%) compared to non-gamers (39%). Additionally, gamers are more likely to be working in a career that they want to be in (45%) compared to non-gamers (37%).

Unsocial

Gamers are thought to be isolative and unsocial. However the study from The University of Massachusetts established that belief to be false. Gamers are more likely to consider friends important than non-gamers (57% of gamers vs. 35% of non-gamers). About 72% of gamers report that they play video games with their friends. Studies have also shown the tendency of gamers to interact with others extends beyond gaming with only 23% of gamers reporting that they watch television by themselves compared to 40% of non-gamers. Studies also examined the importance of family among video game players and found gamers are more likely to have a good relationship with their parents (79% vs. 63%) and consider family a priority (82% vs. 68%) compared to non-gamers.

So clearly the common stereotype for gamers in the United States is flawed. Studies and research have illustrated that gamers include people of every socioeconomic status, ethnicity, and education level in the U.S. The more accurate generalization for gamers is that they can be anyone that you know. It is likely the number of gamers will continue to grow in the United States as the gaming industry overall continues to grow.

Game Addiction in the U.S.

While the U.S. is currently the second largest market in the video game industry and has one of the oldest markets in the world, it lags behind other countries, particularly some in Asia, when it comes to examining the potential addictiveness of gaming. It is only in 2018 that video game addiction started to gain traction as a national topic of discussion in the U.S. This discussion has been spurred by the incredible popularity of *Fortnite* and the concern of parents of the potential effects playing this game will have on their children's academic performance. The U.S. has just started to have conversations about the potential addictive nature of video games. Countries like China, Thailand, Korea, and Japan have been treating video game addiction as a public health issue for over a decade.

Parents and the media are scrambling in the U.S. trying to figure out if gaming addiction is real and if so, how many people in the U.S. have it. The important research quantifying the prevalence of gaming addiction in the U.S. has already been done. Dr. Douglas Gentile, from Iowa State University conducted the most comprehensive study regarding youth and video game addiction in the U.S. in 2009. Gentile's study included approximately 1,200 youths between the ages of 8 and 18. The purpose of the study was to examine national habits among this age group in relation to their video-game habits and determine what percentage of American youth meet criteria for *pathological video game play*.

The chart below illustrates Gentile's findings regarding the frequency of video game play and obtaining mature-related video game content among study participants.

Respondents' Frequency of Playing Video Games

As illustrated approximately 88% of study participants play video games with varying frequency. Boys spend more time than girls (16.4 hours per week vs. 9.2 hours per week). Frequency and duration of video game play among study participants was relatively stable from ages 8 to 13 before starting to drop off. The graph below shows the average weekly amount of video-game play by age among study participants.

Based on study results, Gentile found that about 8% of video game players in the U.S. in this age group exhibited *pathological gaming tendencies*. Gentile made this determination based on study participants' responses to an 11-item questionnaire that was used to identify and quantify pathological gaming behavior. The results of the survey are provided below.

TABLE 2
Percentage of the Sample Reporting Each Symptom of Pathological Video-Game Use

Symptom	Total sample		"Yes" responses only	
	"Yes"	"Sometimes"	Boys	Girls
Over time, have you been spending much more time thinking about playing video games, learning about video-game playing, or planning the next opportunity to play?	21	19	29	11***
Do you need to spend more and more time and/or money on video games in order to feel the same amount of excitement?	8	9	12	5***
Have you tried to play video games less often or for shorter periods of time, but are unsuccessful?	2	22	2	3
Do you become restless or irritable when attempting to cut down or stop playing video games?	2	6	2	1
Have you played video games as a way of escaping from problems or bad feelings?	25	20	29	19***
Have you ever lied to family or friends about how much you play video games?	14	10	17	10***
Have you ever stolen a video game from a store or a friend, or have you ever stolen money in order to buy a video game?	2	2	3	1*
Do you sometimes skip household chores in order to spend more time playing video games?	33	21	40	24***
Do you sometimes skip doing homework in order to spend more time playing video games?	23	19	29	15***
Have you ever done poorly on a school assignment or test because you spent too much time playing video games?	20	12	26	11***

A study participant was considered to exhibit pathological video game playing tendencies if he or she answered yes to six or more of the questions provided in the table above. It was unclear if *"sometimes"* should be counted as a *yes*, a *no*, or something in-between when evaluating survey responses. Therefore three analyses were performed to take this uncertainty into account. In Version A all "sometimes" answers were changed to "yes." This produced a 19.8% pathological gaming rate among study participants. In Version B, "sometimes" were changed to "no." This produced the lowest pathological gaming rate at 7.9% among study participants. Version C changed "sometimes" to be "yes" half of the time and "no" half of the time. This produced a pathological gaming rate of 8.5% and had the highest reliability out of the three versions (meaning it was the most likely to be accurate).

Comparisons of Pathological and Nonpathological Gamers: Continuous Variables

Variable	Nonpathological gamers		Pathological gamers				
	M	SD	M	SD	d	95% CI	p_{rep}
Mean number of years playing video games	5.5	3.2	6.6**	3.2	0.34	(0.12, 0.56)	.98
Mean frequency of playing video games (0 = never, 7 = at least once a day)	4.0	2.3	6.3***	1.1	1.28	(1.16, 1.40)	.99
Mean weekly amount of video-game play (hours)	11.8	12.6	24.6***	16.0	0.88	(0.62, 1.15)	.99
Mean number of video-game rating symbols known	3.4	2.3	4.2**	2.1	0.36	(0.16, 0.56)	.98
Mean grades usually received	6.1	1.5	4.8***	1.9	−0.76	(−1.03, −0.49)	.99
Frequency of trouble paying attention to classes at school (1 = never, 5 = always)	2.5	0.9	3.0***	0.9	−0.55	(−0.78, −0.33)	.99
Overall health (1 = not at all healthy, 4 = extremely healthy)	3.1	0.7	3.0	0.6	−0.15	(−0.34, 0.04)	.95
Frequency of hand or finger pain (1 = never, 6 = almost every day)	2.7	1.2	3.0*	1.3	0.24	(0.01, 0.47)	.94
Frequency of wrist pain (1 = never, 6 = almost every day)	2.7	1.2	3.1**	1.4	0.31	(0.06, 0.56)	.98
Frequency of neck pain (1 = never, 6 = almost every day)	2.9	1.4	3.2	1.4	0.21	(0.00, 0.43)	.91
Frequency of blurred vision (1 = never, 6 = almost every day)	2.7	1.3	2.9	1.3	0.15	(−0.06, 0.56)	.82
Frequency of headaches (1 = never, 6 = almost every day)	4.1	1.5	4.5	1.5	0.27	(0.05, 0.48)	.81
Mean age	13.1	3.0	13.3	2.7	0.07	(−0.13, 0.27)	.66
Frequency of using the Internet to do homework (1 = never, 5 = almost always)	3.0	1.0	3.1	1.1	0.10	(−0.14, 0.33)	.67
Respondents' self-ratings of how much they are affected by violence in the games they play, compared with other students of the same age (1 = a lot less, 5 = a lot more)	1.7	1.0	1.9	1.1	0.19	(−0.05, 0.43)	.93

Pathological gamers were more likely to have been playing video games for more years and play at a greater frequency. Additionally pathological gamers played for twice as long compared to non-pathological gamers (24.6 hours vs. 11.8 hours). Pathological gamers were also more likely to have lower grades and were more likely to have trouble paying attention in class at school compared to non-pathological gamers.

Comparisons of Pathological and Nonpathological Gamers: Dichotomous Variables

Variable	Nonpathological gamers (%)	Pathological gamers (%)	Odds ratio	95% CI	p_{rep}
Has been diagnosed with an attention problem (e.g., attention-deficit disorder or attention-deficit/hyperactivity disorder)	11.0	25.3***	2.77	(1.66, 4.65)	.99
Has felt "addicted" to video games	21.1	65.4***	7.00	(4.34, 11.28)	.99
Has friends who are "addicted" to video games	56.8	77.2***	2.67	(1.56, 4.67)	.99
Has been in a physical fight in the past year	12.3	24.1**	2.28	(1.36, 3.82)	.99
Has a video-game system in the bedroom	40.8	64.4***	2.69	(1.71, 4.22)	.99
Has a TV in the bedroom	62.4	69.0	1.36	(0.86, 2.18)	.81

As illustrated in the table, pathological gamers are more than twice as likely to be diagnosed with an attention problem (25.3% vs. 11%).

When the North American game industry collapsed in 1983 it set the U.S. back several years compared to its Asian counterparts. The Asian gaming industry moved ahead of the U.S. in development overall. Asian countries were faster to smartphones and eSports. A good exercise to predict next what will be big in the U.S. gaming industry is to look at what already exists in the Asian Pacific Region.

Only now is the U.S. waking up to the addictive nature of video games. Due to a lack of knowledge of the problem coupled with inaccurate perceptions of who a video game player may be, treatment options have remained limited. Some deny that the problem exists. Others in need have been unable to find help due to lack of treatment options.

Currently, there are only a handful of treatment programs in the U.S. There are some adolescent wilderness camps in the Mid-West and in-patient rehabilitation programs in the South and West. People are left with zero resources to help their loved ones. Unfortunately, the U.S. has failed to heed the lessons learned by other countries and finds itself with no treatment options for those affected and no legislation to stem the creation of new video game addicts.

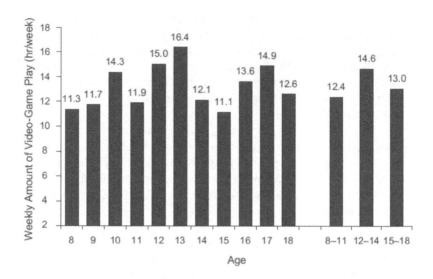

Weekly Amount of Video Game Play by Age

How the industry actually makes money

The fundamental business model of the gaming industry has morphed in recent years. Ten years ago, the industry practiced a common business model of providing goods for purchases. A consumer could purchase a game console and corresponding games directly from producers like Sony or Microsoft or from a third party retailer like GameStop. The consumer purchase of these products marked the end of the revenue stream for the producers.

In recent years, there has been a seismic shift as the industry moved from viewing games as products to viewing them as a service. By viewing games as a service, the entire business model changed. In the old model, developers would typically spend millions of dollars creating a new game and then sell it directly

to the consumers for an up-front price. Consumers who purchased the game could then play it as much as they wanted. In
that model, developers would experience a tremendous amount
of revenue from game sales in the weeks following its release
followed by a sharp drop off shortly thereafter. The consumer purchase of the game typically marked the end of the revenue cycle
for developers.

Growing popularity, accessibility, and capability of the internet
drove two significant shifts in the business model. Game developers could distribute their games directly to consumers over
the internet, which was immensely profitable due to significant
decreases in distribution costs and not having to utilize traditional
brick and mortar stores. GameStop, a traditional brick and mortar
third party provider of video games and consoles, experienced
significant revenue declines as more consumers opted to purchase their game content online directly from the developers.
GameStop eventually had to close 250 of its stores and create a
new business model to survive.

The second shift caused by the internet was that it allowed
developers to provide continuous updates to their games. In the
past, a game would have to be free of glitches before it was released. Occasionally, a game would have serious problems after
it hit the market. The developer would inevitably take a serious financial hit as a result. With the internet, developers could provide
continuous updates to games which consumers could download
directly. The internet allowed developers to provide new content
for consumers without having to release new games.

For their first attempt at the service model, the gaming industry took a cue from the fashion, food and dog care industries. In
recent years, a number of developers of games and consoles have
offered subscription services. Doing this decreased the up-front
cost to the customer. In the past, consumers would have to buy
a game to access the content. Now consumers could "rent" a
game and try it out without ever having to commit to purchasing it. Subscription services have produced mixed results. While
revenue increased overall (subscription revenue was higher than

traditional sales revenue), customer acquisition costs, how much a company has to spend to obtain a customer, were still too high. With many games available to consumers for free, developers who charged customers to play struggled when competing with developers who provided their game for free (i.e. why would a customer pay for something that they could get for free).

Because of the mixed results with the subscription services model, the industry pivoted and implemented a model called *freemium*. This model allows users to download and play games for free. By providing games for free, developers are able to mitigate consumer resistance to paying for access. Consumers can make micro transactions. These are in-game purchases. For example, in *Fortnite* players can purchase "skins" which are just cosmetic changes to their avatar's appearance. This does not do anything to improve the performance of the player and is for cosmetic purposes only. Recently the NFL partnered with *Fortnite* and will release NFL skins for purchase starting in November. The freemium model allows developers to have a steady stream of revenue from consumers through micro transactions instead of one-time lump sum payments from game purchases.

The freemium model turned out to be a tremendous success. More and more game developers have started to offer their games for free knowing that they can generate revenue from micro transactions. *Supercell* is a game developer that produced the hit *Clash of Clans*. In 2015, *Supercell* generated $2.3 billion in revenue, predominately from in-game purchases. King produced *Candy Crush* in 2012 and generated $1.99 billion in revenue in 2017. Like *Supercell*, King's revenue is generated almost entirely from micro transactions as the game is free to download.

While Supercell and King may be outliers, their success has spurred other developers in the industry to switch to freemium models. It is common for people to spend money on customizing their avatars. Gamers are frequently ridiculed by friends and family for wasting money. Surprisingly, the majority of in game purchases are for customization, not to improve performance or odds of winning. Initially developers allowed players to make micro transactions which improved the ability of the player. However the gaming community revolted against this "pay to win" model and stopped playing games that employed such tactics. Paying for cosmetic changes has met no such resistance and is incredibly popular among players. From the perspective of a video game player it may seem strange to spend hundreds of dollars on shoes or thousands of dollars on a handbag.

Video Game Addiction in Asia

South Korea

South Korea is recognized as the Mecca of the gaming industry. It has the fastest internet speed in the world, tens of thousands of internet cafes dedicated to gaming, three channels on television that provide coverage on gaming, and countless tournaments. South Korea is nearing the 20th anniversary of recognizing gaming as a professional sport.

In 1975, a department store in Seoul, South Korea was seeking novel ideas for marketing campaigns. The purpose of the campaign was to increase the number of people who visited the store, thereby increasing sales. The team was aware of the craze in North America around *Pong* and they ordered three to put in the department store. The public went crazy as thousands of people came out to see these strange machine boxes. From this marketing campaign for a department store the video game industry in South Korea born and placed on a trajectory that would make it a world leader for years.

Initial opposition was fierce. Conservative parents feared video games would affect their children's academic performance and the government was concerned that video games would increase criminality. Initially the government sought to use licensure as a means of controlling the video game industry. At the start of 1980 the government only provided licensure to only 43 arcades. Demand for game play far exceeded the licensed capacity. Shortly thereafter hundreds of illegal arcades opened in response to public demand. In March of 1980, the government raided and closed approximately 360 illegal arcades. These raids did little to stem the growth of the gaming industry, as an estimated 20,000 illegal arcades were operating by 1983. Parents were concerned about the academic performance of their children and sought to limit the amount of time their children spent in arcades. They preferred them to go to bookstores to read and study. Ironically unbeknownst to most parents, numerous illegal arcades were located in bookstores behind false bookcases.

Initially, the South Korean gaming industry was import dependent, receiving games and consoles from the United States and Japan. South Korea was behind the U.S. with the prevalence of home computers. South Korean companies started to drive innovation in the computer industry by sponsoring computer classrooms in schools in 1983. This sponsorship program influenced a generation of computer-savvy teens who knew how to program computers and create games. By the end of the 1980s, computers had become common in Korean households. This was due to a convergence of skill and opportunity.

As the computer industry continued to develop throughout the 1980s, arcade and home game consoles dominated South Korean gaming. By 1993, an estimated 25% of households in South Korea had a console. This was the height of game consoles in South Korea as a mass hysteria that game consoles caused seizures destroyed the market. The seizures were eventually proven to not be caused by game consoles, but the South Korean media perpetuated the myth and the console segment never fully recovered.

Advances in computer technology, coupled with the fall of consoles, allowed computers to take the lead position in the gaming industry in the 1990s. In 1998, several additional events coincided to make South Korea's gaming industry what it is today.

End of a Monopoly:

Up until 1998, the South Korean telecommunication industry was controlled by the state sponsored monopoly Korea Telecom. That year, the government started to end the Korea Telecom monopoly and encouraged other companies to enter into the telecommunications industry. In 1998 a new company (Hanaro

Telecom) entered into the industry and determined that Korea Telecom controlled 90% of the dial-up call market. Rather than compete directly against their strength, Hanaro Telecom decided to make a bet that broadband internet would overtake.

Leader in internet speed

Shortly thereafter, the South Korean government decided they wanted to take the world lead in internet speed and connectivity and started to invest significant money into internet capabilities and speed in South Korea. Internet accessibility and capability exploded at the start of 1998 in South Korea. South Korea is still recognized as having the fastest internet speed and being the most internet-connected country in the world.

Rise of PC Bangs

PC Bangs are computer cafes stocked with high-end computers designed for gaming. They are open 24 hours a day and are typically stocked with energy drinks, coffee, and snacks. Users pay an hourly rate to use the computer. Prices were approximately $1.20 per hour. The first PC Bang opened in 1998. By the end of the year there were several hundred PC Bangs in operation.

Asian Financial Crisis

In 1997 Asian countries experienced a significant financial crisis. It started in the summer of 1997 when Thailand was forced to devalue its currency. This caused a domino effect in the region. As the Thai economy faltered other countries in the region (including South Korea) started to falter as well. South Korea's economy continued to worsen toward the ends of 1997 due to several large South Korean companies going bankrupt. Eventually in December 1997 the International Money Fund (IMF) stepped in and helped stabilize the South Korean banking system with a bail-out package of approximately $60 billion. This helped slowly start to stabilize the collapse.

During the Asian financial crisis unemployment in South Korea more than doubled from approximately 3.5% in 1996 to 8.1% in 1998 (over 1.7 million were unemployed). For those that had jobs, there was a lack of stability as the percentage of daily workers and temporary workers increased dramatically. Additionally worker's income decreased 14.2% from 1997 to 1998. Overall the Asian financial crisis left a large percentage of the South Korean labor force unemployed, significant instability for those that were employed, and with decreased incomes. Many workers were left with little money, no work, and nothing to do with their time.

The Spark: *StarCraft*

By the end of 1998 the South Korean gaming industry was primed to explode. All that was needed was a spark. That spark was provided by game producer Blizzard Entertainment with the release of their hit game *StarCraft* (a massively multi-player online role-playing game (MMORPG) where more than 100,000 people can play the game at the same time.) The very nature of MMORPGs lends themselves to being played in a group setting such as a PC Bang. It was an ideal symbiotic relationship. By the end of 1998 there were several hundred PC Bangs in South Korea. A year later the number of PC Bangs in South Korea grew to excess of 15,000. Sales of *StarCraft* quickly exceed one million and eventually reached 4.5 million in South Korea alone. With PC Bangs and *StarCraft*, South Korea developed an infatuation with gaming that was unprecedented and became infused in South Korean culture.

Rise of Professional Gaming

As the gaming industry continued to grow worldwide, developers started to host competitions. As competitions and prize pools increased, a new breed of gamer emerged: the professional. By 2000, thousands of spectators would tune in to watch live competition (eSports was born).

Responding to the growth in popularity of eSports, the government created the South Korean e-Sports Association (KeSPA) in 2000 to promote and regulate eSports. KeSPA manages the broadcasting of eSports, creates new events, provides oversight on the working conditions of professional gamers, and promotes video game playing. KeSPA even supported Nexon (a game developer) to build the first eSports stadium to host official competitions.

With the strong support and financial backing of the South Korean government, professional gamers started to enjoy significant fame and fortune. Lim Yo-han, a professional gamer, married actress and sex symbol Kim Ga-yeon in 2011. More than 150 professional gamers earned in excess of $100,000 in tournament prize money in 2018. Lee Sang Hyeok, who goes by the player name *Faker*, earned $1.175 million playing *League of Legends* in 2018. It is also believed that he was paid another $2.6 million for sponsorships. Professional video game players in South Korea are as famous as professional athletes in the U.S. and Europe.

Growing Concerns:

In the early 2000s as the popularity of gaming was exploding in Korea, concerns started to be raised regarding the potential addictive nature of gaming. These concerns were amplified following deaths associated with gaming. In 2005, Seungseob Lee entered a PC Bang to play *StarCraft*. After playing for 50 hours straight (only stopping for restroom breaks), Seungseob collapsed and died. Friends reported that he was a video game addict who had recently lost his girlfriend and job because of his addiction.

Shockingly, police believe that Seungseob was dead for several hours before being discovered by staff. When the police and paramedics arrived, the other PC Bang patrons continued playing their games as his body was removed. While the public was abuzz about the death of Seungseob Lee, the next death attributed to video game addiction horrified them.

In 2009, a three month old girl named Kim Sa-Rang died from malnutrition. An investigation into her death determined that her parents left her for extended periods of time to go to the local PC Bangs to play video games. Public outrage quickly grew to horror when investigators revealed that her parents were consumed with playing a video game in which they raised a virtual child while their real daughter died from lack of care.

The Government Takes Action

In response to growing public concern, the government conducted studies to determine the existence and extent of gaming addiction among South Koreans. They found that an estimated 10% of the 10-19 year-old population in South Korea was addicted to the internet. Up to 67% of the middle school survey participants started that their primary use of the internet was to play video games. This equates to 700,000 individuals. Other surveys found that up to 50% of Korean teenagers could be diagnosed with *Internet Gaming Addiction*. There are clearly significant deviations in reported prevalence of *Internet Gaming Disorder* between these two studies. The accurate number is probably somewhere in the middle. The South Korean government saw enough from these studies to become convinced that Internet Gaming Disorder was a serious public health issue.

Treatment

Approximately 24% of Korean children diagnosed with internet addiction are hospitalized. The most severe cases of internet addiction among South Korean youth receive treatment at the "Internet Dream Village." This is a thirty day residential treatment program that provides digital detox. During the course of their stay clients have no access to computers, mobile gaming devices, smartphones, or television. Throughout the course of the day they attend psychoeducational and psychotherapeutic groups where they cover topics ranging from gaming addiction to learning how to connect to others in real-time. In addition to therapists the facility also uses "mentors" who stay with the clients 24 hours a day (this is because most of the clients struggle at night time when they normally would be playing video games). After completion of the in-patient program clients return to their homes where they continue to receive therapy on an out-patient basis. The government is vested in providing treatment for their youth. While the services provided such as the Internet Dream Village are good, they need to be expanded to ensure access to treatment for the majority of the population.

Legislation

To try to stem the growth in addiction among the youth, the government sought to restrict internet gaming access. In 2011, the Korean government passed "The Youth Protection Revision Act." This act, which is commonly referred to as the "Shutdown Law" or "The Cinderella Law," forbids children under the age of 16 from playing online games between midnight and 6:00 a.m. The roots of this law trace back to 2004 when civic groups started to grow concerned that adolescents and teenagers were playing video games when they should have been sleeping. While the law was well intentioned it didn't produce the desired effect. Youths were able to find ways to get around the access restriction and still play games during the prohibited time frame.

Video Game Addiction in Asia

Japan

While South Korea may be the Mecca of gaming, Japan is the birthplace. Their history of innovation in the gaming industry is long and storied. Industry standards such as *handheld gaming consoles* and *arcade games for a quarter* trace their roots back to Japan.

While the U.S. dominated the console segment in the 1970s, Japan focused on arcade games. Companies like Sega and Nintendo initially entered the industry by producing high quality arcade games and went on to become the main exporter of arcade games during their golden age. When the North American video game industry collapsed in 1983 Japanese companies took the leadership position. Nintendo, Sega, and Sony released game consoles that were tremendously successful. Japan dominated the worldwide video game industry for the next two decades. By 1986 Nintendo controlled 70% of the console market worldwide. Japanese companies were the leaders in the gaming industry up until the early 2000s.

Japan has set the trends in the industry. In the early 2000s, years before other countries, Japan started to switch from game consoles to mobile gaming. Eventually the rest of the world caught up and has started to switch to mobile gaming. While the rest of the world started to play *Angry Birds* in 2009, Japanese game makers were developing intricate role player games for mobile devices. Reflecting the maturity of the Japanese mobile gaming market, Japan has the highest rate of average

48

revenue per player in the world. Today, mobile gaming remains very popular in Japan with revenues exceeding $6 billion annually. When Japan experienced a recession in the late 2000s, the gaming industry stagnated. Twelve years later, recent signs point to growth in the console market.

Today the Japanese gaming industry is led by mobile devices. Arcades, however, a relic in most other markets, continue to be very popular. As of 2017, Japan had approximately 4,900 large arcades and another 9,000 smaller ones. One reason arcades continue to be popular is that many video game makers (such as Sega) own arcades. These makers have a vested interest in ensuring that there continues to be innovation in the arcade offerings. Japan is no longer the largest gaming market in the world. That distinction belongs to China. However, we expect Japan will continue to innovate for years to come.

Government Action

While Japan has always been a leader in the industry, they have been surprisingly slow to address the potential addictiveness of gaming. In 2003 and 2004, South Korea and China started to take significant steps towards addressing gaming addiction. Eight years later, the first clinic specializing in internet addiction in Japan opened. According to statistics from the treatment facility, 90% of people seeking assistance in combating their internet addiction played online games excessively every day. However it wasn't until 2012 that the Japanese government conducted studies to determine if Internet Gaming Disorder was a problem. A research team from Nihon University conducted a national wide survey of 140,000 students. The government became very concerned as studies suggested that an estimated 8.1% of high schoolers were addicted to the internet (518,000 people). Once the government realized the extent of addiction among high school students it took action. They opened a number of "internet fasting camps." Clients spent time at the camps immersed

outdoors and learned how to connect with humans in reality instead of virtual reality. As the scope of Internet Gaming Disorder
started to come into greater focus, the government expanded the
number of treatment facilities specifically for gaming addiction.
By 2016, there were 28 such facilities.

Legislation

Japan also lags behind other Asian countries in regards to draft-
ing legislation specifically targeting the addiction potential of
video games. The most pertinent law Japan had regarding gaming was the "Act Against Unjustifiable Premiums and Misleading
Representations" which went into effect in 1962. The act was
originally created as a means to fight organized crime by reducing gambling. An unintended consequence of this law was that it
prevented Japanese players from competing, winning and keeping proceeds from participating in eSports. It was ironic that all
eSports competitions lacked players from the country that the
gaming industry was built on. However the law was repealed in
2018 and ushered in the new age of eSports in Japan.

Japan is a land of gaming contradiction. They originally
dominated the global market for game consoles but recently
experienced a decade of declining domestic console sales. Japan
has a healthy and growing arcade business while they are relics
in other countries. They saved the gaming industry, but could not
participate in eSports until 2018. Japan led the gaming industry
for nearly half a century but responded much slower to the addiction potential than every other Asian country we researched.
In spite of Japan's last place position in regards to treatment, they
could potentially become the leader. Gaming addiction treatment hasn't gained traction in Japan because their health system
is based on the *International Classification of Disease*. When the
gaming addiction hit Japan, the current manual was the ICD-10,
which did not include gaming addiction. Thus services were not
provided. With the release of the ICD-11, which does include

Internet Gaming Disorder, Japan could assume another leadership position.

Video Game Addiction in Asia

China

By 2015 China had become the largest and most profitable video game market in the world. The size and scope of China's gaming industry is surprising considering it is relatively young. Gaming started to become popular in the 1990s with the introduction of PC games. At that time, computers were expensive and few households owned one. In response to growing demand for access, internet cafes (similar to the PC Bangs of South Korea) opened. As popularity grew, the Ministry of Information Industry (MII) was formed in 1998 to provide oversight and regulation of the telecommunication and electronics industry. The MII was also tasked with creating initiatives to increase the number of domestically produced online games. Growth in the industry was rapid because it was backed by government initiatives to make gaming more popular.

China's gaming industry was predominately built on PCs and mobile devices. Consoles never gained a significant market share in China due to a government ban on them from 2000 to 2015. The government banned them citing fear that they would have adverse mental and physical effects on children. Despite the console ban, the gaming industry continued to grow in China in the early 2000s. That growth was accompanied by subindustries that supported gaming.

One such subindustry was gold farming. Gold farming is continuously playing a massively multiplayer online game, such as *World of Warcraft*, to acquire in-game currency which can then

be sold in the real-world for money. It may seem crazy to think that people would be employed in such a capacity. By 2005 it was estimated that there were over 100,000 full-time gold farmers in China, predominately from poor inland China provinces. At one point a number of prisons in China had their prisoners working as gold miners for the economic gain of the prisons. Private sector gold miners earned approximately $0.30 cents per hour as gold farmers and routinely worked twelve hour shifts seven days per week.

While the Chinese government initially supported the industry, within a decade they started to become concerned about the potential addictiveness of gaming. In 2002, a fire at an unlicensed internet café killed 25 college students who were playing video games. A number of the victims stayed at their computers ignoring the fire alarms. In 2005, the government issued a report that stated 13% of youth who used the internet were addicted. While the Chinese government was still attempting to quantify the scope of video game addiction they still took action. Initially, to curtail youth access to PC games, the government shut down over 16,000 internet cafes in 2004. That same year, the government opened the first of several hundred "addiction camps" at Beijing's Military General Hospital (more on these in a moment). Several news stories continued to increase the public's fear of gaming. In 2005, one video game player fatally stabbed another for selling a virtual reality sword that was loaned to him. In February 2007, a 26 year old a northern Chinese man died after playing computer games for seven days straight. His parents reported he only left the computer to use the restroom and sleep for a few hours. Seven months later, another Chinese man dropped dead in an internet cafe after ceaselessly playing internet games for three days.

Recognition of Internet Addiction Disorder

China became the first country to officially recognize internet addiction as an official clinical disorder in 2008. According to the Chinese Ministry of Health, criteria for being diagnosed with *Internet Addiction Disorder* (IAD) included staying online for more than six hours per day and having adverse reactions from not going online. Government studies, salacious media stories, and parental fear led to a rapid increase in the popularity of addiction camps. The internet-addiction camps soon got out of hand. In 2006, Yang Yongxin opened a treatment center in Shandong Province where he provided psychotherapeutic services and administered electroshock to his patients. He did this despite not being a psychotherapist or being licensed to use electroshock therapy. He allegedly performed electroconvulsive therapy without anesthesia on patients aged 12 to 30.

In 2009, Deng Senshan (15 years old) was taken by his parents to the Qihang Salvation Training Camp for help with his internet addiction. Deng was an exceptional student and athlete as a child. As a teenager he spent more and more time playing internet games. He lost interest in sports and his grades plummeted. Deng's parents were uncertain of what to do. They were consumed with fear. Approximately 13 hours after Deng Senshan was dropped off at the Qihang Salvation Training Camp, he was dead. He had been beaten to death. A few weeks later a 14 year old boy was beaten to death by a counselor at a different addiction camp in Sichuan.

While the actions of Yang Yongxin (the man who performed ECT on clients) and the deaths in the addiction camps were widely reported, the fear of internet addiction was still very prevalent and alternative treatment options were not readily available. The government eventually passed legislation which forbade the use of electroconvulsive therapy for addiction treatment and prohibited staff from striking patients at the camps. Legislation was drafted which sought to curb internet gaming addiction. A

2010 Chinese law requires players to use their legal names to participate in online games. Game developers were forced to set up time restrictions based on the player's age.

With most of the legislation and addiction camps targeted at teenagers, there were minimal adult treatment options. This left parents of adults with gaming addiction few options. In 2013, a man in China was frustrated that his adult son was unemployed and showed little interest in getting a job. His son preferred to play *World of Warcraft*. Exasperated, the man hired online assassins to kill his son's avatar every time his son logged online. The man hoped that by being repeatedly targeted and killed, his son would grow frustrated and lose interest in the game. While this story is comical, it illustrates how concerned parents in China have become regarding internet gaming and the lack of resources available for help.

Limited Treatment Options

Without viable treatment options, addiction camps continue to be the most utilized modality. Grisly conditions continue to adversely impact those who attend the camps. In 2014 Guo Lingling, a 19 year-old female, died at a camp after being beaten by staff for two hours after failing to ask permission to use the bathroom. In September 2016, a 16 year-old female tied her mother to a chair upon returning home from an addiction camp. Eventually the mother starved to death. The daughter cited camp abuse as a motive for revenge against her mother. In July 2017 a 16 year-old male committed suicide while at an addiction camp by jumping from the roof of his building. Eventually the public became desensitized to deaths in addiction treatment centers. Terrible stories and health concerns remain in the spotlight. In 2014, a Chinese couple was arrested and charged with selling their children to human traffickers so that they could use the proceeds to continue to fund their video game addiction.

In July 2018 the Chinese Ministry of Education released

findings from a survey of 5,000 youths. It found that 17.7% of Chinese teenagers play video games for at least 4-5 hours per day. In August of 2018 China's president Xi Jinping publicly stated that staring at screens too long was to blame for the rise in nearsightedness among Chinese youths.

Video Game Addiction in Asia

Thailand

Thailand is a relatively new and small player in the gaming industry. They are projected to be 20th in the world in 2018 gaming revenue (approximately $692 million). Comparatively, China holds the number one spot in the gaming revenue and is projected to generate 50 times more than Thailand. While Thailand is currently a small player in the gaming industry, they are a leader in Southeast Asia. With a population of 650 million people, Southeast Asia represents 8.6% of the world's population. By 2020 Southeast Asia is projected to have the world's fifth largest economy. As growth in mature markets (China, the United States, and South Korea) has slowed, game developers are shifting their focus to the massive potential of Southeast Asia, with Thailand as the lynchpin.

Thailand's inclusion in this book is not because of its current gaming market size, but rather its projections for continued growth. They have one of the fastest growing gaming industries in the world. The Thailand market is projected to experience annual growth of 15% and reach a market valuation of $2 billion by 2025. To capitalize on the potential of the Thai market, a number of industry leaders are investing in creating the infrastructure necessary to turn Thailand into a world class player.

The two main components of the Thai gaming market are mobile device gaming and PC gaming. The largest market share is held by mobile gaming devices, with a projected $331 million in revenue in 2018. As big as mobile gaming already is in Thailand, it is likely to grow. Only 26.1% of Thai had smartphones in

2015. That number increased to 34.5% in 2018 and is projected to reach 40% by 2020. Additionally, Thai users spent an average of 5.7 hours per day on their mobile devices with approximately 40-50% of that time being spent on social networking and playing video games.

The PC gaming market had approximately a 15%-20% market share of the gaming industry in Thailand in 2017. This represented a 6% increase from 2016. This significant growth in PC gaming is attributed to fierce competition among computer producers that drove down the cost of computers thereby making them more affordable. Overall the growth of the Thai gaming industry is extraordinary considering that the industry did not exist in Thailand until the 1990s. It started when cheap exports and knockoffs of game consoles and video games started to arrive from China.

Government Takes Action

In 2003, the Thai government became the first to take action when they enacted legislation which required all game servers to be blocked between 10 pm and 6 am. However, this measure proved ineffective and was replaced with legislation that limited gaming time at internet cafes. The new legislation stipulated that children under the age of 15 can only play games at internet cafes between 2 pm and 8 pm. Teenagers over the age of 15 are only allowed to play games between 2 pm and 10 pm.

In 2008 an 18-year-old Polwat Chino was in desperate need of money to continue to play his favorite video game *Grand Theft Auto*. Chino's parents refused to give him money to play the game. Chino decided to imitate his favorite game and rob a taxi driver. He purchased two knives and selected his victim carefully. What was initially supposed to be a robbery turned into murder when Chino stabbed the taxi driver to death when the driver started to fight back. After being arrested Chino stated, "Killing seemed easy in the game." Chino also stated, "I needed money to play the game every day." Upon questioning, the man reported his motive for the crime was to see if it was as easy to rob someone in real life as it was in the game. The Thai government immediately suspended the sales of *Grand Theft Auto* in response to the public hysteria that followed the grisly murder. A police spokesperson said, "The police are empowered to immediately arrest shopkeepers if they find any GTA (*Grand Theft Auto*) games on sale."

With growing public concern about the prevalence of Internet Gaming Disorder among the youth, the Thai government commissioned several studies to determine the extent of the problem. A 2013 survey of 20,000 children nationwide found that 15% of the respondents were addicted to video games. With a youth population of 18 million, this equated to approximately 2.7 million Thai youths addicted to video games. The Department of Mental Health and Ministry of Public Health conducted another study to examine the growth rate of Internet Gaming Disorder among Thai youth in the preceding years. They were shocked to learn that the rate of game addiction among youths increased by 300% from 2006-2013. Not only did Thailand have a problem with Internet Gaming Disorder, but it was getting worse. The growing addiction rate was especially troubling because the government found that gaming addiction was associated with adverse effects on health (visual impairment, back pain), academic performance (lower grades and higher rates of absenteeism), emotions (irritability/aggression and homicide), and relationships (family and friends). The government realized that addiction was adversely impacting all major aspects of the players' lives.

In 2015 another survey was commissioned to quantify the extent of gaming addiction. A sample of 295 youths in Bangkok elementary schools participated in the study and answered surveys regarding their video game use and impacts. For the purpose of the study, gaming addiction was defined as maladaptive dependency that adversely impacts the life of the user. The results of the survey were extremely concerning to government officials and the public overall. The survey found that 7.5% of the participants suffered from video game addiction and another 16.6% were in danger of becoming addicted.

Recent surveys estimate that anywhere from 7%-15% of the Thai youth are addicted to video games. Video game addiction has become a health crisis in Thailand in spite of its being a new market. The surveys by the Thai government suggest that Thais have a significant cultural predisposition to gaming addiction. As a result of Thailand being pivotal to the next growth segment in the gaming industry, the Thai will have greater access to gaming than they ever have had before. This access, coupled with an already significant gaming addiction problem, suggests that the number of Thai struggling with gaming addiction will only increase over the next decade.

Treatment options for video game addiction in Thailand are currently limited. As of July 2018 the Institute of Youth Mental Health is providing treatment to 429 children diagnosed with gaming addiction at an inpatient and outpatient level of care. There are a number of private facilities that provide treatment options for video game addiction. However their cost is substantial and not affordable to many Thai. Most efforts are currently geared towards providing educators and parents with tools to protect their children from developing gaming addiction and how to identify children that are at risk. Additionally there is no formal organization or body that provides oversight and regulation of the

treatment of video game addiction treatment industry. The growing impact of video game addiction among the Thai will continue
to grow worse until actions are taken to provide appropriate treatment to the masses.

Manipulative Psychology

In 1957 Vance Packard startled the American public with his best-selling book, *The Hidden Persuaders*. It revealed and explained, sometimes in lurid terms, how Madison Avenue exploited consumers by triggering and manipulating emotional responses to words and images to evoke images in the readers to increase sales of specific products (and political candidates).

Behavioral science insights have often been used to position products or services for commercial gain. That is no less true for the game design industry.

Consumers have an almost limitless number of video game options. Developers routinely spend millions to successfully bring a game to the market. In the past, developers relied on an initial flurry of sales following the release of a game. That business has changed. Many game developers have slashed the prices of their games. Others offer them for free. The biggest fear for developers is creating a game that no one plays. By offering free games, developers are able to get more consumers to try them. This model is called *freemium*: free to play with an option to pay for premium content (this was discussed already). At first glance, this strategy seems risky. After all, the game developers invest a substantial amount of money. Why would they take the risk that might not recoup their investment? As it turns out, developers were not taking much of a gamble. They designed games so that they were addictive. It has been very good for revenue.

Persuasive Technology

The video game design industry is built on the principles of a relatively new discipline called *persuasive technology,* which is the use of technology to change consumer behavior through social influence and persuasion. B.J. Fogg, the founder and director of the Stanford Behavior Design Lab, is the father of persuasive technology and is commonly referred to as "the millionaire maker" due to the successful employment of his techniques by his former pupils (one of whom co-founded Instagram). Persuasive technology is employed by many companies but is rarely discussed, as they do not want consumers aware of the fact that they are being manipulated.

Facebook utilizes persuasive technology. They generate revenue from selling ads. Pricing is dependent on the number of users that are online. Facebook has successfully employed persuasive technology techniques to increase the amount of time users spend on Facebook, thereby increasing what they can charge advertisers. One technique Facebook uses is the continuous feed. This requires users to scroll to find whatever they are looking for, thereby increasing the amount of time that they are on the site. By having more users on for longer periods of time, Facebook is able to charge advertisers higher rates.

The National Football League (NFL) is similar; their advertising revenue has a direct relationship with the number of viewers. During the 2016 regular season, a 30 second advertisement slot cost a couple hundred thousand dollars. A 30 second slot during the Super Bowl cost $5million dollars. Why was CBS able to charge so much more for this game? Simple; there were 100 million viewers. Companies were willing to pay more because the knew their advertisements would be seen by more people. Eyeballs on Super Bowl ads are common knowledge, but the public has been outraged to find out that they are being manipulated by Facebook and other companies.

The premise of persuasive technology is to create digital environments that meet people's basic drivers such as social connection and the desire to feel competent. Describing the potential for persuasive technology in game design, B.J. Fobb said,

> *Video games, better than anything else in our culture,*
> *deliver rewards to people, especially teenage boys. Teen-*
> *age boys are wired to seek competency. To master our*
> *world and get better at stuff. Video games, in dishing out*
> *rewards, can convey to people that their competency*
> *is growing, you can get better at something second by*
> *second.*

There are three factors of persuasive technology associated with changing a customer's behavior: motivation, ability, and triggers. 1) People are motivated by social acceptance. They are even more motivated to avoid social rejection. 2) Ability: digital products should be easy enough so that consumers do not have to work too hard. 3) Consumers need to be triggered to play the game. This can be accomplished by external prompts (alarm clock ringing to wake you up in the morning). Eager to use persuasive design, game design companies turned to an unlikely profession for help in creating addictive games: psychology

Rise of the User Research Lead

John Hopson, who has a PhD in brain and behavioral science, penned a paper titled "Behavioral Game Design in 2001." He discussed how to design video game features to increase their addictiveness. Hopson covered "How do we make players maintain a high, consistent rate of activity" and "How to make players play forever." Hopson stated, "This is not to say that players are the same as rats, but there are general rules of learning which apply equally to both." Impressed by the potential applications Hopson suggested in his paper for video game design, Microsoft hired him. Hopson helped with the development of Xbox Live (Microsoft's online gaming platform) He also worked on the development of popular games like *Halo 3*, which went on to win the "Most Addictive Game of the Year" award in 2007.

Spurred by the success of Microsoft, other game design companies hired psychologists to work as "user research leads." Psychologists work with the production team and run experiments with volunteers who play the game and provide feedback. The psychologists analyze data from the experiments and suggest adjustments to keep players engaged. A series of surprises and rewards make it very difficult to stop playing. Amy Jo Kim, the CEO of ShuffleBrain and a renowned social game designer stated, "Nobody cares about your smart idea; they care about whether something is going to help the game sell a lot."

Psychological Modalities

In his influential paper, Hopson made a reference to rats in a cage. He was referencing the work of B.F. Skinner, a psychologist who conducted experiments. He famously studied the behavior of animals in a box (he placed rats in a box with a lever that dispensed food every time the rats pushed it). The box eventually began to be referred to as the "Skinner box." After some time in the box, the rats began to associate the "behavior" of pushing the lever with the "reward" of a food pellet. They learned that any time they wanted food all they had to do was push the lever. The reward reinforced the behavior, thereby increasing the likelihood of the rats continuing to push the lever. During the course of his experiments, Skinner realized that he could increase certain behaviors in the rats and decrease others by choosing which to reinforce.

Lag legend has it that one day while Skinner was running his experiment that he was running out of food pellets. Skinner started to ration the pellets so that they would last the day. This fortuitous shortage of pellets led to the expansion of Skinner's model to include reward schedule. Up until that point, Skinner either rewarded a behavior every time or never rewarded it. Skinner learned that by varying the reward schedule, which is how frequently the rats were rewarded for engaging in a particular behavior, the rats started to act differently. Various reward schedules are provided below:

Continuous: reward every time for engaging in the desired behavior

Fixed ratio: reward is given after performing "x" number of times

Fixed interval: reward is given after "x" number of time has passed

Variable ratio: reward is given but the "x" number changes every time

Variable interval: reward is given by "x" amount of time that needs to pass is always changing

Skinner's experiments showed that if you design the right box you could improve the control of behavior. At the end of the 20th century a group of psychologists realized the applicability of Skinner's work to video game design. Skinner learned that if you wanted to get the rat to push the lever continuously you should employ a variable reward schedule. This left the rats in state not knowing how many lever pushes were needed to get the reward so they were much more likely to continue to push it than if they pellet came on a continuous or fixed schedule.

Farmville

One of the first games purposely designed to be addictive was *FarmVille*, which was created by Zynga as a Facebook app. *FarmVille* was released in 2009 and quickly became one of the most popular games in the world. In it, players tend to a small farm and raise crops and livestock. Players advance through the game by harvesting crops at a specific time which are then sold for in-game currency. For instance, if you planted a crop of corn in the morning, you needed to return to the game by mid-afternoon to harvest your crop. If you didn't return within the appropriate time frame, you risked losing your crop. Crops that were harvested were then sold for in-game currency which could be used to purchase additional acreage, tools to make harvesting easier, and a variety of decorations.

The graphics of the game are rudimentary and there is no significant change of the routine in the game. As players progress, they simply get bigger pieces of land or they can use in-game currency earned from harvesting crops to decorate their farm. A typical field in *FarmVille* consists of a grid that is a 14 x 14 box plot of land. In each of these boxes, players plant crops. Remember that the in-game currency is generated from harvesting and selling crops. The user earns money if they harvest their crops when the time is appropriate and then plant another crop. This requires three mouse clicks per square. One click to harvest the crop, one click to prepare the land for the next crop, and one click to plant the next crop. Three simple clicks of the mouse does not seem like much. Remember though that the grid is 14 X 14. That means for every harvest and planting, a user needs to click the mouse approximately 600 times. Sounds like a rat in a box.

While other game designers purposely made games addictive, Zynga took their design to a whole new level by focusing on the social relationships of gamers. *FarmVille* was designed so that in-game advancement was very difficult without having in-game neighbors. Players were encouraged to invite friends and family to join the game and become their in-game neighbors. Neighbors could help with taking care of each other's farms and livestock. The game allows users to send each other gifts, post bonuses for help wanted, and post updates on Facebook. This was brilliant marketing by Zynga, as it taped into human's innate sense of social obligation. When users would log onto Facebook, they would see that their neighbors sent them gifts. This produced a feeling of social obligation to respond in kind, thereby increasing the number of people actively engaged in the game. At its height of popularity, approximately 80 million people were playing *FarmVille*. In hindsight, it appears that so many people were playing *FarmVille* because so many people felt obligated to play. Users could use real currency to make in-game purchases which would allow them to progress through the game faster. While it may seem outlandish that players would buy fake tools to tend to their fake crops, Zynga generated over $1 billion from in-game transactions in 2011 alone. That is a fantastic return for a game that cost a few hundred thousand dollars to make.

Casinos & Loot Boxes

Casinos were the first industry to employ Skinner's discoveries. His research was ideally suited for slot machines. In the 1970s, 50% of casino revenue came from slots. Today, 70-80% of casino revenue is generated by slot machines and up to 80% of the floor space in casinos are devoted to them. Years ago, slot machines provided rare payouts. They paid out on approximately 3% of spins. Over time slot designers augmented their design to increase payouts on up to 45% of spins. This change in payout schedules was based on Skinner's discovery regarding reward schedules and influencing behavior. Game designers learned that if they rewarded gamblers more frequently and in smaller amounts, the length of time playing would increase. The longer someone plays, the more the casino makes. Modern slot machines pay out more frequently and in smaller amounts, thereby increasing the time people play. The design of smaller and more frequent payouts is referred to as "drip feed games." One slot machine designer said that "Some people want to be bled slowly."

Video game design companies witnessed the success of slot machines in the casino industry and employed similar techniques. While the video game industry doesn't include slot machines in their games, they created the *Loot Boxes*. These boxes contain sought-after items (advanced weapons, stronger armor, cooler customs). Players could earn keys to open these boxes through game play. Alternatively, gamers could buy (using real money) keys from in-game stores that would open them up. Loot boxes, like slot machines, provide sought-after items on an algorithm basis. This ensures that gamers keep buying loot boxes, thereby increasing revenue for the industry.

Some game designers took loot boxes a step further. A Chinese game, *ZT Online*, uses treasure chests instead of loot boxes, but the concept is identical. Players use keys to open the treasure boxes which may or may not contain items that they want. These virtual keys for virtual prizes are purchased with real money. To further drive business, game designers eventually included a daily prize to the player who opened the most treasure chests each day. Individually players would routinely open over 1,000 treasure chests on a daily basis, only to learn that someone usually opened more than they did. It turns out that there is no shortage of obsessive people, especially those that have been scientifically manipulated.

In the casino industry, the casino always has an advantage in every game that they offer. This is where the adage "The house always wins" comes from. Over the course of time casinos will inevitably make money from gambling because they have a statistical advantage. The smaller the advantage a casino has over players the better the odds of winning are for players. For instance in Blackjack casinos have a very small statistical advantage. Depending on the casino, gamblers generally have up to a 48% chance of winning on every hand.

Roulette is another popular casino game. In it a plastic ball is put onto a wheel with numbers and colors. Players bet on where the ball will end up. The safest bet is to pick a color (Black or Red). Players have a 47.4% chance of winning with this bet. On the opposite end of the spectrum players can elect to bet on a single number between 0-36. The odds of winning on this bet drop to 2.6%.

Slot machines are incredibly popular and take up the majority of the floor space in casinos. However, they also happen to have some of the worst odds of winning. Overall players have about a 40% chance of winning. The combination of slot machines popularity and odds significantly in favor of the house make slot machines generate a lot of revenue. In fact slot machines generate more revenue than all other casinos games combined. On rare occasions people win jackpots on slot machines with a typical payout between $8-$33 million. But the odds of that happening are one in 50 million.

Now players typically don't complain about the odds in the casino industry. They understand that the casinos have an advantage over them. It is public knowledge and readily acknowledged and discussed publicly by the casinos themselves. Alternatively, game design companies historically attempted to keep the odds of winning highly sought after items in loot boxes secret. It wasn't until the Chinese government mandated game design companies to disclose the odds in 2017 that these odds became public knowledge. The odds were bad to say the least.

Players Unknown's *Battleground* was developed and published by PUBG Corporation, which is a subsidiary of Bluehole. It was released in 2017. In the game players fight against other players in a battle royale of up to 100 players in a last man standing deathmatch. Players Unknown's *Battleground* has several types of loot boxes. Some can be purchased for free by using battle points earned from performing well in the game. Others can be purchased with real world currency. It is good that players can earn loot boxes for free. However Players Unknown's *Battleground* limits the number of free boxes that a player can open to six per week. Only one in 10,000 loot boxes have incredibly rare items (such as aviator goggles or a checkered bandana). With the cap of six free boxes per week this means a player can expect to get one of these rare items after playing for 80 years. Alternatively, players can purchase loot boxes which have better odds in getting highly sought after items. This option would only take several thousand dollars and five years. Players Unknown's *Battleground* deserves credit for publishing their loot box odds. However it is eye-opening to see how bad the odds are of actually winning.

Another tactic game designers borrowed from the casino industry was creating *fake currency*. People spend more when they use credit cards or debit cards than they normally would if they had to pay in cash. They typically spend less when they pay in cash because they are able to see the actual cost of their purchase. Casinos realized that by using poker chips, players would become desensitized to the value of money, thereby increasing the amount they were willing to bet. Many video games utilize in-game fake currency. Some games use gold coins, others use rupees, and still others use *gils*. By creating their own currency, video game designers are able to separate between costs in real life and costs in the game.

Game designers created confusing exchange rates that further muddle the water. Instead of using standard exchange rates of 1:1, game design companies started to use complicated exchange ratios so players are not entirely sure how much they are spending. For instance, the currency of a game may be gems. A player can spend $7.99 to buy 60 gems, which they the player can then use for in-game purchases. Now let's pretend that a player decides to purchase an upgrade shield for 23 gems. How much does this equate to in real life dollars? The combination of fake currency and confusing exchange ratios increases in-game micro transactions (the shield cost $3.06, if you were wondering).

Another tool used by game designers to make games more addictive is *augmenting the progression* of the player. New players rapidly progress initially. It is common for players to advance through several levels in the first few hours of playing. However, as they progress advancement starts to slow. Advancement could entail having to spend hours on mundane tasks (such as catching 500 fish). As progression slows, gamers start to anticipate and crave each new advancement. Requiring a significant amount of work to move to the next level is beneficial for the game companies. With players spending more time playing to advance, companies can sell more advertisements (Barack Obama famously paid for in-game advertisements during the 2008 presidential campaign). Alternatively, game companies can offer players the option to make in-game purchases to advance faster.

World of Warcraft

World of Warcraft is a massively multiplayer online role-playing game that was released by Blizzard Entertainment in 2004. Players paid a monthly fee to play the game and at its peak had 12 million subscribers. By 2017 it has grossed over $9.23 billion in revenue. World of Warcraft has been a massive success to say the least. A decade and a half after its release an estimated five million people still play World of Warcraft.

Since its release there have been discussions regarding the addictiveness of World of Warcraft. The International Journal of Mental Health and Addiction published a study looking at the addictiveness of the game in 2010. 438 players from the United States and Canada participated in the study. The study focused on answering two questions:

1. What do players say about video game addiction

2. What percentage (%) of players believe they are addicted to World of Warcraft

The participants answered a questionnaire which focused on demographics, hours spent playing daily, types of games played, and their views on video game addiction. The study found some troubling statistics.

• The average player spent 5.5 hours per day playing video games

• 44% of players reported that they were addicted to computer games

• 62% of players believe that video game addiction is real

• 73% of participants had scores that fell into the category "frequent problems, may be developing an addiction"

• 6% of participants had scores that placed them in the category "most likely have or are developing an addiction"

The study also included quotes from the participants. They were quite eye-opening.

"Whenever I am depressed or wanting to escape from the real world into something I can manage and control I will resort to playing video games."
"I don't look forward to any prolonged time away from my online friends, even to spend time with friends I have in real life."
"I feel like I can't really stop playing the game. It's become more like an occupation or obligation than something optional at the end of the day if I have free time."
"Amazingly, not playing for a few days can send me into withdrawal, similar to my old vice, caffeine addiction."

     World of Warcraft's history and success have made it ideal to study video game addiction. While the game may not have been intentionally designed to be addictive, certain human elements lend themselves to addiction. The community aspect of the game involves human interaction (even if it occurs in a digital space). Humans are social creatures that crave connection. Playing the game may tap into the human nature to find a calling. Players may feel that the community depends on them. In the game players must choose to join one of two competing sides. They also are allowed to guilds or groups. Not being present for other members or your group can produce the feeling that you have let your community down.

    Fogg talked about how humans are hardwired to seek competency and eventual mastery. One of the main components of *World of Warcraft*, and other games as well, is character advancement. Players are driven to improve their character's level or skills. In addition to the choice of which side, groups, or guilds to join, players are allowed to customize their character. In therapy this is called the right to self-determination. When a client, or a video game player, gets to make decisions on what they want to do or who they want to be they are much more likely to feel engaged in the process. By being able to customize their characters players are much more likely to experience heightened engagement.

    Scarcity is an important component of game design. As discussed earlier one of the reasons loot boxes are so popular is that they contain rare items. For some games these items can improve the players performance while others allow the player to customize their character's appearance or outfit. In *World of Warcraft* items can be purchased for gold coins that are earned through game play. Players can earn gold by spending hours doing frivolous tasks like killing creatures. This is referred to as gold farming.

Gold Farming

Initially players gold farmed to earn gold to buy items. However eventually players started to sell the gold they earned to other players who did not want to spend hours killing creatures. This led to a new industry as companies started to open who sold gold that they farmed in the game. Workers would spend hours every day collecting gold which they then sold to players. At its height there were over 100,000 workers in China working as gold-farmers. Additionally Chinese prisoners were forced to gold farm for hours every day. Eventually gold farming was made illegal but the practice still continues. Gold farmers spend up to twelve hours per day farming gold which then they sell for around $80. This equates to $25,000 per year. Former gold farmers struggle to quit and seek real-world employment. Addiction is incredibly high among gold farmers.

One final aspect of *World of Warcraft* that lends itself to addiction is *random drops*. At random intervals equipment and gold are dropped by defeating enemies. However players never know when this is going to happen. The only one to get these drops is by playing the game. Players never know if the next orc they kill will drop something they want or the 10,000th orc. This uncertainty can lead to loss chasing which is common in gambling. People that struggle with gambling addiction always think that "the next one" will be a winner. They believe that "it has been so long so they are due." This is a false but powerful belief. *World of Warcraft* players are susceptible to the belief that maybe the next enemy they kills will drop something they want. Just one more round.

Fortnite

To say *Fortnite* is popular is an understatement. It was released by Epic Games in 2017. In the game players can team up to save the world from zombies, fight in a battle royale to be the last person standing, or to create anything they want on an island. Fortnite has become a cultural phenomenon. In response to its popularity, Epic Games created the first *Fortnite* world cup which was hosted in New York. The price pool was $30 million making it the biggest e-sports event in history. A look at the psychology behind the game design helps explain its popularity.

Decades of research has shown that making measurable progress towards a goal motivates people. People feel excited and engaged when they are working towards something. *Fortnite* has been designed to provide specific and motivating feedback about progress towards goals. For instance players can see how close they are to unlocking a feature of the game. Additionally players receive in-game notifications as they make progress towards goals.

A specific type of progress in *Fortnite* is called "endowed progress". A good example of this would be a gas station that gives you a free oil change for every ten that you pay for. This is called the "endowed progress effect". Humans usually want to complete goals that they have made some progress towards. In video games, it is not uncommon for players to initially make progress towards goals which they weren't even aware existed. In *Fortnite* players can open a chest that they come across in the game. They may then receive a message which says "Searched 1 of 4 Treasure Chests." Up until this point the player not have even realized that this was a goal. But all of a sudden they are 25% complete towards the goal. They will most likely keep going now to try and complete the goal.

Two other psychological principles used in the design of *Fortnite* is rarity and achievement. Unlike other games there is no visible ranking in *Fortnite*. Players are able to upgrade their characters by either purchasing skins or by spending time to level up their characters. For players upgrading your character shows how you stack up against other players in the game. *Fortnite* has seasons. Each season lasts three months after which players' levels are reset. The faster a player can upgrade at the start of a season the better they are assumed to be.

Video game design has changed over the years. Today video game companies employ workers who are versed in psychology to aid in the design of the games. It can cost hundreds of millions of dollars today to successfully bring a game to market. Most of the games today are free to play or only cost a nominal amount. The true profit engines of games today are in-game purchases. To help ensure a significant return on investment, game design companies today utilize psychological principles which increase engagement and spending tendencies of players. While game companies may never have intended to create addiction, the game mechanisms such as rapid advancement, self mastery, engagement, and artificial scarcity have predisposed players to becoming addicted.

Recognizing Addiction

Although video game addiction is real, it is sometimes difficult to distinguish between what normal video game play and what video game addiction looks like. Recognizing the signs and symptoms of video game addiction is paramount to parents, administrators, and therapists. Parents do not need to be experts to determine whether they think their loved ones may have an issue with video games. Likewise, therapists do not need to be experts on video game addiction to screen for and identify video game addiction. This chapter plus the glossary in the back of this book are meant to arm parents and therapists with aids in identifying those who are struggling.

Building Rapport

Building rapport is incredibly important whether you are a parent or a therapist. *Rapport* is a noun that is used to describe a close and harmonious relationship in which the members feel understood by each other. Rapport encourages the back and forth flow of information, attitudes, opinions and feelings. Looking back at Frank's story with his South Korean client at the Rutgers Counseling Center illustrates the importance of rapport. Initially Frank was making very little progress in getting the client to open up. Frank would ask questions and the young man would give one to two word answers. He slouched back, had his arms crossed, and avoided eye contact. Overall he was clearly disengaged. However when Frank asked the client what level his character was in *World of Warcraft* he lit up. He sat up and leaned forward. He started speaking rapidly and with emotion.

The entire tone of the conversation and session changed dramatically. The client started pouring out information. Frank is not and never has been a *World of Warcraft* player. Some of his friends played so that is how Frank knew about character levels. The key takeaway from that story is that Frank knew "enough" to give the client confidence that Frank understood his passion.

When dealing with someone whom you suspect may have a problem with video games establishing rapport is critical. Serious gamers may have spent years feeling misunderstood. They may feel that their parents and teachers "just don't get it." They may be frustrated and angry that others tell them that it is ridiculous to spend real money on customizing their character's avatar in a game. Whether you are a parent, administrator, or a therapist, it is important to have at least some base understanding of games. Become familiar with the glossary provided in the back of this book. Refer to it when you hear video game terminology you don't understand. Use interactions with video game players as an opportunity to learn. This can be a powerful role reversal for the video game player who may have been told for years that their hobby is childish. Additionally, here are some general questions you can ask if you are unfamiliar with the specific game or games they play. Is the game single player or multiplayer?

1. Is it storyline based (does it have specific levels and a determined end)?

2. Is it a massive online battle arena (MOBA) or a massively multiplayer online role-playing game (MMORPG)?

3. Does the game use character levels to signify achievement (how skilled you are)?

4. Does the game have e-sports events?

5. How do you level up in the game?

6. What level are you?

7. Are there loot boxes?

These are enough questions to get the dialogue flowing. It is most important not to pretend to be an expert in the different video games (unless you really are). Rather the important thing is to establish rapport. These questions will help illustrate that you have enough knowledge of gaming for the player to start sharing with you. Inevitably they will say something that you do not understand. That is okay. Ask the player to explain it to you. This further solidifies the expert role-reversal and increases engagement.

One important final note on establishing rapport. Never pretend to know something that you do not know. For example let's look at a therapist working with a client who struggles with Cannabis Use Disorder. The initial focus is on building rapport. The therapist appears to know what they are talking about and the client starts to feel understood. However at one point the therapist asks "Are you injecting marijuana on a daily or weekly basis?" In this instance the client immediately is aware that the therapist does not understand. You smoke or eat marijuana—you don't inject it. There is significant damage to the rapport that has been built. When dealing with video game players access your ignorance. Admit what you don't know and ask them to teach you. Think about something that you are really passionate about. How does it feel to be around other people who either share your passion or at least are genuinely interested in learning more about it. At the end of the discussion thank the video player for teaching you.

Screening

For therapists who work with clients it is important to have a screening tool. Research has shown that there are few characteristics that can be used to automatically eliminate who is at risk for developing video game addiction. People of all ages, races, gender, education level, relationship statuses, and socioeconomic statuses play video games. The best practice is to include a question regarding video game play into the standard assessment or intake. The question can be as simple as "Do you play video games?" If the individual reports not playing video games then move on. However, if they do report that they play video games it is appropriate to ask some follow up questions. Typical questions include focusing on frequency of play, duration of play, and last reported play. If the individual reports playing frequently for extended periods of time then it is time to move onto a formal assessment for video game addiction. Dr. Gentile from Iowa State University created an 11-item questionnaire to help in screening for video game addiction.

1. Over time, have you been spending much more time playing video games, learning about video game playing, or planning the next opportunity to play?

2. Do you need to spend more time and money on video games to feel the same amount of excitement as other activities in your life?

3. Have you tried to play video games for shorter durations of time but have been unsuccessful?

4. Do you become restless or irritable when you attempt to cut down or stop playing video games?

5. Have you played video games as a way to escape problems or negative feelings?

6. Have you lied to family or friends about how much you play video games?

7. Have you ever stolen a video game from a store or a friend or stolen money to buy a video game?

8. Do you sometimes skip household chores in order to play more video games?

9. Do you sometimes skip homework or work in order to play more video games?

10. Have you ever done poorly on a school assignment, test, or work assignment because you spent so much time playing video games?

11. Have you ever needed friends or family to give you extra money because you've spent too much of your own money on video games, software, or internet game fees?

Individuals who respond "yes" to six or more of these questions are most likely struggling with video game addiction. However even if someone only answers "yes" to a handful of these questions, it is imperative to look at the impact video games are having on his life. This is one of the few screening tools available for video game addiction. However, it is not without its limitations. For certain individuals some of these questions can result in a false negative. For instance, a 19-year-old who is not currently in school nor working will not experience video games affecting his performance in school or work (isn't currently doing either). This questionnaire is meant to be a starting point for further discussion. In the example of the individual not in school or working, a more appropriate question would be are they not in school or working because they are spending all of their time playing video games?

Differences Between Those Addicted and Not Addicted to Video Games

In his research Gentile looked at differences between pathological (addicted) and non-pathological gamers. His research and findings continue to lead the field of video game addiction. His work shed light on some significant differences between addicted and non-addicted gamers. In his research he looked at continuous variables and dichotomous variables. Continuous variables occur on a spectrum. For instance a question that asks you to rate your satisfaction on a scale between 1 (very unsatisfied) and 5 (very satisfied) is measuring a continuous variable. Alternatively dichotomous variables can only have one of two answers. For example, a question that asks "do you drink coffee: yes or no" is measuring a discontinuous variable. Gentile's research measured both continuous and dichotomous variables. Table 1 below illustrates some of the differences between these groups and continuous variables.

Comparisons of Pathological and Non-pathological Gamers: Continuous Variables

Variable	M	SD	M	SD	d	95% CI	prep
Mean number of years playing video games	5.5	3.2	6.6nn	3.2	0.34	(0.12, 0.56)	.98
Mean frequency of playing video games (0 5 never, 7 5 at least once a day)	4.0	2.3	6.3nnn	1.1	1.28	(1.16, 1.40)	.99
Mean weekly amount of video-game play (hours)	11.8	12.6	24.6nnn	16.0	0.88	(0.62, 1.15)	.99
Mean number of video-game rating symbols known	3.4	2.3	4.2nn	2.1	0.36	(0.16, 0.56)	.98
Mean grades usually received	6.1	1.5	4.8nnn	1.9	0.76	(1.03, 0.49)	.99
Frequency of trouble paying attention to classes at school (1 5 never, 5 5 always)	2.5	0.9	3.0nnn	0.9	0.55	(0.78, 0.33)	.99
Overall health (1 5 not at all healthy, 4 5 extremely healthy)	3.1	0.7	3.0	0.6	0.15	(0.34, 0.04)	.95
Frequency of hand or finger pain (1 5 never, 6 5 almost every day)	2.7	1.2	3.0n	1.3	0.24	(0.01, 0.47)	.94
Frequency of wrist pain (1 5 never, 6 5 almost every day)	2.7	1.2	3.1nn	1.4	0.31	(0.06, 0.56)	.98
Frequency of neck pain (1 5 never, 6 5 almost every day)	2.9	1.4	3.2	1.4	0.21	(0.00, 0.43)	.91
Frequency of blurred vision (1 5never, 6 5almosteveryday)	2.7	1.3	2.9	1.3	0.15	(0.06, 0.56)	.82
Frequency of headaches (1 5 never, 6 5 almost every day)	4.1	1.5	4.5	1.5	0.27	(0.05, 0.48)	.81
Mean age	13.1	3.0	13.3	2.7	0.07	(0.13, 0.27)	.66
Frequency of using the Internet to do homework (1 5 never,							

5 5 almost always)	3.0	1.0	3.1	1.1	0.10	(0.14, 0.33) .67
Respondents' self-ratings of how much they are affected by violence in the games they play, compared with other students of the same age (1 5 a lot less, 5 5 a lot more)	1.7	1.0	1.9	1.1	0.19	(0.05, 0.43) .93

Source: Gentile, D. (2009). Pathological video-game use among youth ages 8 to 18. Psychological Science 20(5).

Note that Table 1 illustrates some interesting trends. Addicted gamers typically have played for more years, with greater frequency, and for longer duration of time when they play. They struggle more to pay attention in school and perform worse academically. Additionally they report higher rates of hand or finger pain, neck pain, blurred vision, and headaches. Gentile also looked at dichotomous variables (either yes or no variables). The results are provided below in Table 2.

Comparisons of Pathological and Non-pathological Gamers: Dichotomous Variables

Variable	Non-pathological gamers (%)	Pathological gamers (%)	Odds ratio	95% CI	prep
Has been diagnosed with an attention problem (e.g., attention-deficit disorder or attention-deficit/hyperactivity disorder)	11.0	25.3nnn	2.77	(1.66, 4.65)	.99
Has felt "addicted" to video games	21.1	65.4nnn	7.00	(4.34, 11.28)	.99
Has friends who are "addicted" to video games	56.8	77.2nnn	2.67	(1.56, 4.67)	.99
Has been in a physical fight in the past year	12.3	24.1nn	2.28	(1.36, 3.82)	.99
Has a video-game system in the bedroom	40.8	64.4nnn	2.69	(1.71, 4.22)	.99
Has a TV in the bedroom	62.4	69.0	1.36	(0.86, 2.18)	.81

Source; Gentile, D. (2009). Pathological video-game use among youth ages 8 to 18. Psychological Science 20(5).

ICD.6 The WHO and APA update their manuals to reflect changes in diagnoses. Updates include removing diagnoses (homosexuality was recognized in the first edition of the DSM and then removed nineteen years later in the second edition of the DSM), updating criteria for current diagnoses, and adding new diagnoses. Both organizations have weighed in on Internet Gaming Disorder, but they have some disagreements. The APA initially was spurred into weighing on IGD in 2007 when it received a request from the American Medical Association (AMA) to include the disorder in the next edition of the DSM. While the APA initially supported the inclusion of Internet Gaming Disorder in the DSM in 2007, they eventually backed off of that position stating that further research was needed. In 2013 the APA released the 5th edition of the DSM and reported that IGD as a "Condition for

Further Study". In 2018, the WHO released the 11th edition of the ICD and included Gaming Disorder. In this edition the WHO included Gaming Disorder.

ICD-11 Gaming Disorder Criteria:

1. Impaired control over gaming intensity, duration, termination, context
2. Increasing priority given to gaming to the extent that gaming takes precedence over other life interests and daily activities
3. Continuation or escalation of gaming despite the occurrence of negative consequences

A diagnosis of Gaming Disorder is contingent upon adverse consequences in various roles and responsibilities (family, social, educational, personal, or occupational). An individual needs to exhibit the behavior for at least 12 months. However, the diagnosis can be given sooner if all three criteria are met and the symptoms are severe and causing significant impact to the individual's life.

Even though the APA started considering video game addiction earlier than the WHO, it is not surprising that the WHO acted first. Globally, video game addiction is a much more accepted disorder than in the U.S. China, Thailand, South Korea, and Japan have treated gaming addiction as a serious public health crisis for over a decade.

DSM 5 criteria:

The APA refers to video game addiction as *Internet Gaming Disorder*. While the ICD-11 lists three criteria for diagnostic purposes; the DSM-5 uses nine. The DSM-5 criteria are provided below with corresponding explanations. To be diagnosed with Internet Gaming Disorder an individual must meet at least five of the criteria above for at least 12 months.

Pre-occupation: relates to spending a significant amount of time thinking about playing video games. In order for this criterion to be met the individual would have to think about playing video games throughout the course of the day.

Withdrawal: withdrawal refers to the experiencing physical or psychological symptoms when a person is not engaging in a behavior. Common withdrawal symptoms for gamers include irritability and restlessness. For this criterion, to be met the individual needs to experience withdrawal symptoms when they are not playing the game.

Tolerance: tolerance is characterized by increased playing time (A common occurrence for problem video game players is playing for longer than they intended or being unable to stop once they start).

Unsuccessful attempts to stop or reduce: this criterion is characterized by an inability to stop playing video games or having failed at reducing the amount of time spent playing overall. For this criterion to be met an individual would have to exhibit an inability to reduce or stop playing despite intentional efforts.

Loss of interest in other hobbies or activities: this is characterized by a decrease in engagement in other recreational activities (like softball, guitar, painting, or reading comics).

Excessive gaming despite Problems: this is associated with an individual who continues to play games despite experiencing significant negative consequences. Such consequences can include adverse health experiences such as not enough sleep, financial consequences from spending too much money, and professional consequences such as routinely being late to work or school.

Deception: deception is characterized by covering up the extent of video game playing or lying to others about it. A common occurrence among adolescent and teenage gamers is pretending to go to sleep at night only to play video games in their bedrooms.

Escape or relief from a negative mood: this criterion is characterized by engaging in gaming as a means to escape negative feelings such as depression or anxiety. Individuals may also play games to escape from having to deal with problems in the real world, preferring instead to seek shelter in an alternative virtual world.

Jeopardized or lost a relationship, job, or educational or career opportunity: this refers to losing or putting in serious jeopardy important relationships or job/school opportunities. An individual that is in jeopardy of failing out of school or does fail out of school due to excessive gaming would easily meet this criterion.

Internet gaming disorder can be mild, moderate or severe. Severity is dependent on the degree to which normal activities (work, relationships, hobbies) is disrupted by playing video games. Those with severe IGD will have more severe loss of relationships as well as severe impacts on school or career performance.

Primary, secondary or comorbidity

The DSM has specific language that can cause confusion. Three such terms that require clarification are primary, secondary, and comorbid. A primary disorder is a disorder that is the main source of disruption in a patient's life. Common psychiatric primary disorders include Major Depression and Bi-Polar Disorders. Secondary disorders arise as the result of a primary disorder. For instance, a person who carriers a primary diagnosis of Bi-Polar Disorder with Manic episodes might have a secondary diagnosis of sleep disturbance. The sleep disturbance is secondary because it is caused by the manic behavior. Theoretically, if we address the mania then the sleep disturbance should be resolved. Comorbid are primary disorders that occur at the same time: a substance abuser that also has an anxiety disorder.

With the inclusion of Internet Gaming Disorder in the section for disorders that need further study, research has started to focus on trying to determine if IGD is primary or secondary. Research is also focused on determining the comorbidity of Internet Gaming Disorder. Some found evidence that suggest Internet Gaming Disorder is a primary disorder. The main argument that IGD is a secondary disorder is focused on individuals using gaming as a means to escape or as a coping strategy. The evidence suggesting Internet Gaming Disorder is a primary disorder is stronger than the evidence against it. Researchers are much more confident regarding the comorbidity of Internet Gaming Disorder. Common comorbid conditions include depression, obsessive-compulsive disorder (OCD), attention-deficit hyperactivity disorder (ADHD) and anxiety. As depression and Internet Gaming Disorder have similar risk factors (lack of social support and loneliness), it makes sense that these conditions are so often comorbid. Answers to the question regarding Internet Gaming Disorder as a primary or secondary disorder (I believe it is a primary one).

Further research should help clarify comorbid disorder combinations. While additional clarity is appreciated, it is not necessarily important. From a therapeutic perspective, practitioners focus on treating the whole person, not one disorder at a time. When a person presents themselves for treatment and exhibits symptoms of depression and Internet Gaming Disorder, the therapist won't only treat the depression first. If the therapist focuses on treating only the depression, then the gaming could become worse and impact progress with depression treatment. Therapeutically it does not matter which disorder came first because at the point of treatment, all disorders are present and need to be treated in combination.

Addicted and Non-addicted Players

One of the core tenants of addiction is that the addiction has some sort of significant adverse effect on the individual who struggles with addiction. Gentile's research found significant differences between those who struggled with video game addiction versus those who were not addicted. Do not automatically rule out of the possibility of video game addiction for someone based on their age, race, gender, or socioeconomic status. The main focus when evaluating anyone for video game addiction is on establishing rapport. Once this is established start to probe for additional information. You do not need to be an expert on video games in order to effectively screen and diagnose for video game addiction. Access your ignorance and allow the individual to teach you about video games. Use resources like this glossary to look up terms you are not familiar with. Look for the impact video game play is having on their individual lives. If someone is experiencing a significant adverse impact on his life as a result of video game play then use the questionnaire to gather additional information.

A Story of Recovery

In January of 2019, I sat down with Matt, a student at Rutgers who has been in recovery from video games and other digital addictions for a few years. We talked for a couple of hours and I learned an incredible amount from him. He agreed to write up his story and then answer a number of written questions. While every person who struggles with these disorders is different, there are some common problematic signs and helpful solutions. I am extremely grateful to him for his efforts here. – Frank Greenagel

My name is Matt and I'm a digital addict. On the face of it, I'm a pretty ordinary college student. I was raised in Northern New Jersey, I go to Rutgers University, and I study physics. I live in the dorms with a bunch of my friends, and I spend most of my free time hanging out with them, or my girlfriend who I met through a tutoring job. I get good grades (straight A's so far, fingers crossed), I'm involved in research, and I'm planning to go to graduate school after my senior year. I say 'pretty ordinary' because I would estimate that I'm a bit more successful and happy than the typical college student. I say 'digital addict' because that means all that stuff will be ruined if I start playing video games again.

Let me start from the beginning. I grew up an intellectual and sensitive child, aka a huge nerd. I don't think I received an above-average dose of bullying, but I do know that I felt awkward and uncomfortable around other kids my age. Also, for as long as I can remember, I've enjoyed playing video games, watching TV, and messing around online. As I grew older, and my adolescent discomfort intensified, I started to use these activities to procrastinate when I wanted to avoid homework and to make myself feel better about awkward social situations at school, in addition to playing during my spare time. I experienced some consequences from spending so much time online, but these were never that bad because while I was living with my parents and everything I needed was provided for me. When I left for college, I began spending more and more time online until it occupied most of my waking hours. After my freshman year, my grades had dropped below the cutoff for my scholarship, and that summer my parents found me unwilling to do anything except sit in my room and play video games. On the advice of my therapist, my parents gave me an ultimatum; I had a month to take certain specified steps towards getting my life together, or I couldn't live with them anymore. I didn't take this seriously, and did nothing. About a month after my deadline had passed, my parents held an intervention for me. They told me that they thought I was addicted to my electronics, and that I had the choice between homelessness and a rehab. I chose not to be homeless, and that night I was in a rehab in Delray Beach, Florida.

I was a very sheltered kid, and it was a shock to suddenly find myself living among drug addicts and alcoholics, many of whom had been homeless, convicted, and chronic relapsers. More shocking still was how much I could relate to them. Not only did I use my computer like they drank and did drugs, I also did everything else I enjoyed to excess, tried to manipulate and control those around me, and couldn't deal with my emotions, just like all of them. The longer I spent there, the easier it was to admit that addiction had been my problem the whole time, and the more hope I had that I could actually stay sober. This was important, and I still say that my treatment center was instrumental to my staying sober, but I also say that getting out of rehab was when the real work began. I discovered that, even though I was resolved to quit video games completely, my addictive tendencies could manifest themselves in all of my interactions with computers. I found that, in a bad frame of mind, I would even scroll through Google Images compulsively. I had to figure out how to stay sober without a treatment center holding me accountable and shielding me from temptation.

The answer I found was a Twelve-Step program, and it's

worked for me ever since. Although the program I participate in is designed for substance abusers, and I struggled for a long time with feeling like I didn't belong, I found people willing to help me regardless of my past. My therapist and my twelve-step sponsor helped me work out my boundaries around electronics, but this work turned out to be less important for my sobriety than finding emotional stability through the Twelve Steps. What also helped was becoming heavily involved with the local recovery community, an experience that gave me a sense of purpose and belonging while I worked low paying jobs to support myself and took community college classes to get my GPA back on track. I made a boatload of friends during this period, which I feel was crucial to building my self-confidence. All told, I spent two years in Florida before moving back to New Jersey when I got into Rutgers, and I wouldn't change a minute of it. Cheesy as it is, I needed that time to find out who I was, and develop the emotional maturity that's helped me stay sober since.

I came to Rutgers, and moved into the Rutgers Recovery House, where I've been for the past two years. Living around other people in recovery is important to me, even if they don't have the same addiction, because I feel like I relate with them on a deeper level than non-addicts. Being in the Recovery House also affords me regular access to a therapist, who I see to maintain my mental health. Another benefit of the house is that there are always fun, sober activities going on, which can be difficult to find on a college campus. This is what allows me to have fun while still maintaining a heavy academic workload and participating in research. Finally, in order to stay sober and keep all the things I've earned along the way, I actively participate in a Twelve-Step program; I attend meetings, work the Twelve Steps with a sponsor, and try to be of service to others in and out of the program. The past four years have completely changed my life, and today my present has never looked brighter. As an addict, I wanted to pass up on life; today, I wouldn't miss it for the world.

Q: **You mentioned the consequences. Can you expand on them?
(mental, physical, financial, job, school, legal, friends, family)**

A: To answer this question, I'll try to paint a picture of where I
was at during the lowest point of my addiction. Keep in mind that
this is the lowest point I sunk to, the final point of a progression
that lasted almost a decade, so at other times I was not nearly so
bad as I describe below.

My mental health was probably the most significant consequence. I constantly craved stimulation, either from a computer
or another outside source, and I felt miserable whenever I wasn't
experiencing any such stimulation, and I had no idea how to
pull myself out of this loop. Towards the end of my abusing
electronics, there were very few things that would stimulate me
more than getting online, and as a result, I left my room very
little. My primary concern was the next time I could get onto my
computer, and how I could stay on uninterrupted for as long as
possible. During a binge, I ignored everything but my bladder
and hunger pangs (which were also quieted by Adderall). Game
GUIs were easier to interpret than the signals from my own body.
Being online felt like being in a pleasant haze, and jumping into
interactions with the real world felt oddly intense. After a long
binge, things like the sensation of depth, the light of the sun, or
the feeling of another person touching me were all disorienting.
Once or twice I had borderline hallucinatory experiences where I
saw objects in the real world as game objects, like treasure chests
or checkpoints, which disappeared when I gave them a second
look. It was only when I logged into my computer or my phone
that I felt comfortable.

Physically, I completely stopped taking care of myself. I didn't
bathe or shower for days on end, and I think I brushed my teeth
maybe half a dozen times in the final year. When I began seeing a
dentist for the first time after getting sober, I had too many cavities
for them to count on the initial visit. I had over 25, all told. My
diet consisted on what I could eat with one hand while holding
my smartphone in the other, without any preparation required, so

it was mainly junk food. While at school I eventually became too lazy to go to the dining hall, even though it was very close, and I would mostly eat out of a vending machine in my dorm. When I came home, I would subsist on snacks from the pantry and only ate full meals when my parents would make them, and even then they had to ask me multiple times to come and eat with them. I was definitely underweight, and towards the very end I began to experience dizziness on standing which I now suspect may have been due to malnutrition. I would stay up until 4 or 5 am every night, regardless of what I had to do in the morning. If I didn't have to do anything, I would wake up around 1 or 2 in the afternoon, and spend the entire day in bed on my laptop unless I got up to get food, took my laptop somewhere else for a change of scenery, or I was forced to do something by my classes or my parents.

Financially, I had nothing going for me. I had no job and refused to get one, no matter how much my parents begged or threatened me with consequences. I knew getting a job would mean more responsibilities, and therefore less time to get online, so I avoided one like the plague (I took the same approach to getting my driver's license). I never took up any form of online gambling or pay-to-play games, because my parents had access to my bank account and would have noticed the charges. Online shopping was a serious part of my behavior online, but I would very rarely buy anything. I would simply go to an online store, fill a cart with designer goods on deep discount, and close the window without checking out. The funds allocated to me by my parents were one of the few things I took seriously at that time, although I had no such qualms about the money they paid for me to go to college. My parents also must have spent a fortune on data overages while I was in high school, which I never considered.

I wasted my first year at college. I was going to a good school on a scholarship that paid a significant portion of my tuition. I was completely capable of passing all these classes, but simply didn't care to put in the effort that they required. I am very intelligent, and I thought I could skate through college on my wits and the goodwill of my professors the same way I handled high school (during which I relied heavily on my parents, and consistently performed below my potential anyway). In my first semester, I was taking two morning classes, and I found myself simply unable to wake up in time to attend. I dropped one midway through the semester, but took a D in the other because I didn't bother to check whether or not I was failing. The next semester, I had three C's on my transcript, primarily as a result of turning in assignments late or not at all. This took my GPA below the cutoff to retain my scholarship. I justified this by telling myself I had merely miscalculated, that if I had only known that a C translated to a GPA below the requirement I would have gotten B's instead. I was completely in denial that it was a problem. The constant feeling of achievement I got from playing games felt like a sufficient replacement to me.

My relationship with my friends deteriorated over the year I spent at school. Although I made many friends at the beginning of the first semester (I don't think I've ever had much of a problem with social anxiety), by the end of the second I had lost most of them because I was more interested in spending time on my laptop than maintaining contact with them. In high school, I stood a girl up because I lost track of time playing a video game, and after that I acted as if I was allergic to making plans. There were a few people who were still interested in going to the trouble of hanging out with me, and I scrupulously hid any and all indications of my addiction from them, lying as much as I needed to in order to keep them in the dark. To replace real-life relationships, I satisfied myself with online replacements. I never had online buddies I played games with; I think that would have been healthier than the route I chose. Instead, I constantly watched YouTube and Twitch videos of Let's Plays, videos that show someone playing a game and providing commentary. I would watch these videos religiously, getting to know the personality of the commenters, and learning more about them as I watched the games. They essentially acted like one-sided friends for me. I felt like I was getting to know them, without any of the intimacy of letting them get to know me. It was the ultimate 'safe' friendship.

My family life was awful, and had been increasingly bad several years before this point. My parents wanted me to do well, succeed, and take responsibility for myself, and I would have none of it. We argued often, and the summer before I went to rehab we had shouting matches on a daily basis. At least once, our fighting became physical when my father attempted to take my laptop from me by force. I didn't care what they wanted for me, because all I wanted was to spend as much time online as I could. My younger sister was traumatized by the constant fighting in our home, and at one point walked out of school in the middle of the day and wandered through a local park because she didn't want to return home. When the police were called to our house to take her description, I just shut myself up in my room and refused to help. To this day, the emotional harm I did to my family is one of my biggest regrets, but by this point I was using the internet and video games to numb out my concern about their feelings.

Q: **How old were you when you knew it was a problem?**

A: It's difficult to describe my thoughts during active addiction. My memories are foggy, I was deep in denial, and I've spent so long trying to understand my behavior during that period that sometimes I don't know the difference between how I felt, how I said I felt, and what I've been told I felt. At the beginning, I didn't know I had a problem, and at the end, I knew I had a problem but didn't know how to stop. Where exactly I crossed that line, I can't say for certain. It might be most accurate to say that part of me always wanted to stop, and part of me still doesn't.

Even in high school, I remember being confused by why everything seemed so difficult for me, why I was struggling to handle situations that my peers seemed to sail through, and feel like I must have been able to connect the dots between my performance and my behavior. I considered the benefits of quitting when my parents brought them up to me, and attempted to cut down on my use occasionally. I quit one video game in particular which I spent many hours on after I decided I was too obsessed with it. I also completely deleted all the games on my phone after I found myself not paying any attention in class during high school. I still watched videos on my phone, though, so that boundary did nothing. The insane part was that I considered that boundary still in place, so I didn't watch any videos on my computer for months, even though watching them on my phone was clearly no improvement.

When I was in college, I remember going to bed telling myself that tomorrow was the day I was going to get my shit together, tomorrow was the day, then reach for my laptop the second I woke up. Suddenly the day was over, I had spent it all online, and I would go to bed wondering what was wrong with me. There was a moment when, I think while watching a video, I seriously thought, "Maybe I'm a video game addict." I never addressed the thought, I just let it float away and stayed online. Despite having that thought, when my parents accused me of the same thing, I would always argue back. I might have been able to admit to myself that I had a problem, but I couldn't contemplate stopping. I needed months away from a computer to even consider the possibility that I could actually quit. Living in the real world 24/7 felt like a radical thought at the time. I was so deeply in denial that I had almost no self-awareness, because although I was sacrificing everything I held dear to my addiction, it was the only thing that made me feel good about myself, even briefly. This is what I think of when twelve-step programs talk about being powerless.

Q: **Looking back, how old were you when you think the problem was evident (but you were either unaware or in denial)?**

A: I think that the first stage of the problem was evident as early as my eighth grade year, because that was when I began trying to hide my use from my parents. I would play a game on the home desktop, and whenever I heard somebody coming, I would hit a couple hotkeys to minimize the window so only a Word document with a half-written essay or something like that was visible. Eventually my parents caught on to this strategy, but I don't think they put the puzzle pieces together. I think that the big switch at that point was that I was willfully trying to avoid my responsibilities using the computer, without caring about the consequences. Whereas before I was only playing for fun (when I feel good, I play), at this point I also began playing for escape (when I feel bad, I play). This is the beginning of when getting online became my reaction to every stimulus in my life.

Q: **Did your parents, sister, friends or teachers recognize it was a problem?**

A: The running theme was that while everybody around me was sure I had some sort of issue, nobody was sure exactly what was my problem. At various points in my life, I had been labeled with ADD, ADHD, autism, Asperger's, social anxiety, and depression. I definitely have ADHD, but it's now well managed with medication (more on that below). The others were all off the mark, although I was definitely exhibiting signs of depression. I know it was not clinical depression, however, because those symptoms disappeared rapidly when I was removed from my laptop and phone. However, just trying to figure out what I should be diagnosed with kept my parents off the track of my addiction for a long time. Even though when we would fight, they would yell that I was addicted to my screens, I don't think they believed it until the summer they sent me to rehab. They told me later that during that summer, they began thinking of my problem as addiction and all of the uncertainty they had before suddenly made sense. I'm not sure what my little sister thought before I got sent to rehab, but I know I made her life hell enough for her to tell that something about me was off.

I always hid my addiction from my friends and teachers where I could. Towards the end, some of my friends in college caught on to how much I was lying to them (I only learned this from talking to them afterwards), but they didn't really investigate further. My teachers were aware that I was performing below my potential, but I don't think any of them really caught on to why. A teacher in my first semester of college told me that I was clearly the smartest student in the class, but I was getting grades towards the bottom of the curve. She asked me why, and I don't remember how I answered, so it was probably a lie. I have received feedback like that from many teachers throughout college and high school, so it was not a surprise to me at that point. I was comfortable not doing my best, because my priorities were elsewhere.

Q: **Why do you think it got worse when you went to school?**

A: While I was living in my parent's home, they never allowed me to fully act out on my addiction. They would always make sure I got up and went to school, that I was fed, that I took my medication, and that I got to appointments on time. If they saw me spending too much time online, they would force me to get off and spend some time on something else. They also were able to monitor my grades in high school online and could tell when I wasn't turning in assignments, and remind me to complete them. I resisted all of these attempts to interfere with my downward spiral, and we argued about them frequently.

When I left for college, all of that changed. I became completely responsible for all of the above, and I was able to decide how much time I spent on my devices. At first, I was taking care of myself reasonably well, but as the months went on I began spending more time on electronic entertainment. Eventually, the majority of my waking hours were spent online, I fulfilled none of my responsibilities, and my grades dropped drastically. It was only when I came home for the summer and my final grades were mailed to my parents that they became aware of how bad my situation had become. Essentially, when I went to school, I was given the freedom to let my life crumble around me.

Honestly, I think that was one of the things that helped me get sober the most. While I was at my parents house, no matter how much time I tried to spend online, they wouldn't let me completely fail, and nothing too bad would ever really happen. Since they weren't letting anything really bad happen to me, I had no motivation to change. Going to school allowed me to really be fully faced with the consequences of my actions, and that's what made me willing to try to change.

Q: **When we talked in person, you told me about your roommate and how he had a problem too. Are you willing to talk about that and also to discuss what happened to him?**

A: When I went to college the first time, my first roommate and I got pretty close with one another. We were both pretty far from home, so we confided in each other and became good friends. We had very similar habits, in that we both spent most of our time in our dorm room, on our laptops. He wasn't as into video games as I was, but he spent a lot of time on *Reddit* (something I'm thankful that I never picked up). I used him to justify my behavior a lot; whenever I wondered if I was online too much, I would look over and see him doing the same thing. He had friends, and a girlfriend, and he seemed to be doing all right mentally, so I figured that if he was okay, then so was I. I used these types of flimsy justifications constantly in my active addiction to assure myself I was all right. He also gave me access to his HBO account, which I used to watch about 40 hours of Game of Thrones in three days during the week of my final exams. That was one of the precipitating events that led to me going to rehab a couple of months later.

I think I was in Florida for about 9 months before I was able to contact him again. He was curious why I was no longer going to that school, and I decided to be honest with him about going to rehab for digital addiction. He said that made a lot of sense, because he had been worried that the TV binge he enabled during finals week had been a factor in me leaving school. I was able to let him know that it wasn't his fault for allowing me access, since I was so addicted by that point I would have spent that whole time online anyway. In return, he revealed that he was never the picture of mental health I imagined.

He said that he'd struggled with depression for all of our freshman year, and spending all that time online had been a big part. He had used my presence to justify that behavior to himself, the same way I had used his. We had been enabling each other without realizing it. During his sophomore year, after the summer I went to rehab, the depression only got worse. He attempted suicide by jumping off the roof of a dorm building, but survived. I was shocked when he told me this, but when I thought about it, I don't know if I should have been. I was in such despair at the end of our freshman year, I don't know how far away I was from doing the same. After he got out of the hospital, he went to a week-long therapeutic retreat for depression and took the rest of the semester off, but now he was going back to school. I remember feeling a little jealous that he only went for a week of intensive therapy, while at that point I had been in treatment for months. Still, he sounded very positive and happy over the phone, so I was glad he was getting help, and it made me feel better that I hadn't been the only one struggling with those issues.

Fast forward about six months, and I was on the phone with a couple other friends I had met at that school. I mentioned that I was happy my old roommate was doing so well, and there was silence on the other end of the line. Hesitantly, they told me that he had died. At the time, they didn't know how it had happened, but I was instantly convinced it was suicide, which I later confirmed. Learning about his death was surreal. In recovery-heavy communities like Delray Beach, hearing stories of relapse and death is a part of everyday life, but this was the first time someone I was really close to had died, so it impacted me deeply. At the same time, it had been a long time since I spoke to him, longer still since I'd seen him, and I was far away from everything that was going on, so I also felt very detached. To this day, my feelings about his death are complicated. I say that I honor his memory by living not as he did, but as he would have wanted me to. To a certain degree I blame myself, because I don't think there was anyone around him who knew what he was going through as well as I did, but I try not to because I think he wouldn't want that from me. I hope he would have wanted me to focus on helping the people that are still here and struggling with this addiction, which is part of the reason I agreed to write this.

Q: **You went to a traditional alcohol and drug treatment program in Florida. Did anyone there specialize in internet gaming disorders? What was your treatment like? How long were you there**?

A: My primary therapist in that treatment center had experience working with cross-addicted patients in the past (those who abused internet and gaming in addition to alcohol and drugs) but I believe that I was the first patient who came to treatment solely for digital addiction. There were two more who came to treatment shortly after me, though. Although that therapist had no formal training on digital addiction (to this day, I'm not aware that any formal training program exists), he had enough experience to be a great help to me. For me, dealing with the specifics of my addictive behaviors was less important than addressing the underlying mental and emotional issues that led me to that in the first place.

I followed essentially the same program as all of the patients in treatment for substance abuse. I completed four months of inpatient. For the first two months I attended three therapy groups a day every weekday, and I spent the next two months in their vocational program, during which I attended two therapy groups every weekday and spent the rest of the day looking for a job.

After I found a job, I spent two months in their IOP, which consisted of one therapy group each weekday. At this point, I started
going to school part time. After IOP, I attended one group a week
as part of outpatient therapy, which lasted about seven months,
while living in sober housing (mine was a sober dorm program).
This was pretty standard for addicts of all kinds who attended
their treatment program.

As far as treatment of my technology issues, I did not touch a
computer for the first two months. I feel that this 'digital detox'
was extremely helpful in clearing my mind and allowing me to
reflect on my behavior. The next two months, I was allowed to
use desktop computers owned by the treatment center, but only
to look for employment. Occasionally during this time I accessed
various other sites on these computers, and if this was discovered
(or if I outed myself, which I did at points because by this time I
wanted to get sober) my use of these computers would be restrict-
ed for a period of time. After I found a job, my therapist recommended that I purchase a flip phone rather than a smartphone,
which I did. I used the desktop computers for work-related re-
quirements and to apply for school. Once I got into school, I used
computers at the treatment center and on campus to complete my
homework, but did not use computers otherwise.

I did not purchase a laptop until about eleven months into
sobriety, again at the recommendation of my therapist. It was a
ChromeBook, which doesn't have a hard drive, because I thought
that not being able to download Hearthstone even if I wanted to
would be helpful. In retrospect, that didn't really make a difference for me, since there are so many games and distractions
available over the internet anyway. The first weekend I had it, I
binged several nights in a row watching music videos on You-
Tube, and I worked with my therapist to set boundaries around
my use. These boundaries have definitely shifted and changed
throughout my sobriety (sometimes becoming looser, sometimes
more restrictive) as needed to maintain a healthy lifestyle, but I
generally try to discuss these changes with a therapist or Twelve-
Step sponsor before making them. For example, I stopped watch-

ing music videos and any YouTube videos that were not required for school after that night. It definitely took a few months until these boundaries were firm enough and my recovery was strong enough to be comfortable having unrestricted access to the internet without fearing a binge. I was very glad I continued to see a therapist one-on-one on a weekly basis while I was figuring out how to manage my computer use.

Q: Did you play games on a console, personal computer or phone?

A: I never owned a console, but I played on a PC (desktop and laptop) and smartphone (and, when I was younger, a Blackberry-style phone). I never owned a console, and was never really interested in getting one because I could get everything I wanted from computers and phones. Playing on a PC also allowed me to hide my gaming from my parents because I did my homework on a computer, so they could never be sure of what I was actually doing. Also, on PCs and phones, there were enough free-to-play games that I could amuse myself for a very long time without ever spending money. I also watched a lot of YouTube videos and Twitch livestreams of gaming, streaming videos of TV and web series, browsed online stores without buying anything, read humor articles, looked up random things on the web, and watched porn, all of which were free, and all of which distracted me in the same way as video games.

Wen I got very deep into my active addiction, doing only one of these things at a time was no longer sufficiently distracting for me, so I would open multiple tabs or windows and do many things simultaneously, just to keep my interest from flagging. I would open a gaming video, then I would open another tab and start online shopping because the 15-second ad was too much for me to sit through, and I would flip back and forth between the two whenever there was a dip in the action in the video. I would play one video game while listening to a podcast about

another game. I would open porn videos on two or three different tabs, mute them all, play my own music in the background,
and cycle through the open tabs; when I got bored of one video,
I would click a link to a new video, switch to an open tab while
it was loading, and by the time I cycled back to the first tab the
new video would be on an interesting scene. At times I tried to
manage my technology use by watching something on my phone
while getting work done on my computer, and inevitably accomplished nothing. Constantly novelty was the name of the game,
and I was working as hard as I could to mainline it.

Q: **What kind of phone do you have? What do you use it for?**

A: I own a flip phone, with a physical 12-button keyboard, and
I use it for texting, calling, and setting alarms. Once in a while I
take a picture, but not often because the camera isn't very good.
I thought this would be a real hardship for me, but I knew that
no matter what, my sobriety had to come first in my life, and if it
took using a flip-phone that was a small price to pay. It was kind
of a hassle initially, but now that I'm used to it, I wouldn't really want to go back, because I find myself much less distracted
by it than a smartphone. I'm currently on my third or fourth one
(unfortunately, they aren't as durable as everyone assumes), and I
intend to continue using them until they stop getting made.

Q: **Do you use computers and the internet today?**

A: I do use computers and the internet today, I own a laptop, but I
have strict self-imposed limitations on the way I use electronics. I
have found that one of the most effective ones is to check in with
someone before every time I use a computer, calling or texting
them to describe what I will do before I do it. The point is not
for that person to police my actions, but to give me a chance to
consider what I'm doing and check if I can really justify this deci-

sion to myself. If it's something I've done many times before and have confirmed is within the boundaries of appropriate use, like doing homework, I just send a text, but if it's something unusual or could potentially go off the rails, I try to call someone beforehand.

Q: What kind of activities do you have to avoid on a computer? How did you make that decision?

A: The one hard and fast rule I use is that if I can give myself a good reason for going on a computer (and entertainment is never a good reason), and can back that reason up to someone else, then it's allowed. Mainly, I use my computer for school, work and work-related projects, checking my email and calendar, and planning events which will occur in the physical world (like finding directions, for example). I only look at streaming videos or news articles when they are specifically required for a class. Occasionally I shop online if I cannot find something, but I try to only go on when I know I am going to buy something in that sitting, in order to avoid my pattern of digital window-shopping. I don't stick to these rules all the time, because I still have an addict inside me trying to get away with as much as they can, but when I do stick to them, I am able to use computers without fear of binging.

I never use video games, and now never view social media, entertainment articles, music streaming, torrenting websites pornography, and online dating, among others. I have always drawn a hard and fast line at video games, for the three years I have been in recovery, but most of the others boundaries I have had to set through trial and error. It's really not possible for me to predict what will trigger a binge and what will not until I have tried it, but if I do find myself using electronics compulsively I have to step back, take a look at what I'm doing, and seriously consider if I need to set a boundary on it, almost always discussing my deliberations with someone I trust. This is how I set my boundaries around streaming music, entertainment videos, pornography, and dating websites; I tried to use them normally, stayed on for longer than I had intended, and decided that any potential benefit wasn't worth the cost to my sobriety.

Unfortunately, I have found that I can't be as hard-and-fast with my recovery as former substance abusers I know, because with the amount of time I spend interacting with electronics, binges are almost inevitable. What's more important for me is picking myself up afterwards, making sure I don't continue the binge, identifying what the problem was, and taking steps to find a solution. The difference between the pretenses at trying to manage my abuse during active addiction, and maintaining my sobriety now, is that I learn from my mistakes instead of trying the same thing over and over again, and that now I'm willing to go to any lengths for my sobriety, even if it means giving up something I don't think I can live without. I felt I would be totally unable to give up streaming and downloading music, and I found it possible and now my life is better for it. I had exactly the same experience when I gave up porn. I find that at its best, my sobriety is a gradual weaning off process, where I slowly winnow my use of electronics down to the bare minimum. Every time I find myself called upon to give up another behavior, I wail that my life will be miserable without it, and every time I give it up, I find my life gets better.

Q: **This is your third semester at the Rutgers Recovery House. Students are traditionally there because they are in recovery from alcohol and/or drugs. How have the staff and students treated you?**

A: Although my issues were new to many staff and students at Rutgers, I have always been given respect and support for what I deal with. Some people have had questions about computer addiction, and what exactly my boundaries are, but after this long staying sober I have more experience fielding those questions. I know that there are some people who don't understand the things

I deal with, but at this point I remind myself that I don't need everyone else to understand me perfectly, so long as I know what my own limits are. All I need at this point is for people to respect my program, and I have not had any cause for complaint on that front.

Sometimes, I struggle with the fact that other people in the house do play video games, binge-watch media, and other behaviors I don't participate in. Sometimes that makes me feel left out, but the nice thing about living in a house with so many other young people in recovery is that there are always other things going on that I can participate in, which don't involve electronic media or substance abuse. For me, this is what makes living in the Recovery House worthwhile.

Q: **Your problem is with video games and other aspects of computers and the internet. You never had an actual problem with alcohol or drugs? Do you use them?**

A: Both of my parents are in recovery for drug and alcohol addiction, and from a fairly early age I was convinced that I had the genetic predisposition, and I would become an alcoholic if I began to drink. Because of this, I avoided experimenting with alcohol and drugs like other kids my age, but I had no such qualms about using video games and the internet. Because of this, throughout all of high school and my first year of college I had a total of two sips of beer (both times just to fit in at a party) and smoked weed twice. However, while I was in college, I did abuse my prescription of Adderall in order to stay awake longer and play video games. I used the excuse that since it was prescribed for me it didn't matter what time I took it, so I would take it late in the evening so that I would stay alert for longer. I never enjoyed the effect of that drug by itself, I only used it to focus more on my gaming experience.

Today, I do not use substances, for three reasons. The first is that given my non-substance addiction and a long family history of substance abuse, I think it's likely that I would develop a problem with substances. The second is that I have no interest in drinking or using substances. It has simply never looked very appealing to me. Third, and most important, I maintain my sobriety by working a Twelve-Step recovery program, and the one I'm involved in is intended for substance abusers. If I were to use alcohol or drugs, I would feel obligated cut myself off from that source of support, and I have no desire to do that.

Q: **When you meet someone new, how long do you take before you tell them you are in recovery? How do you go about telling them? What is the typical reaction?**

A: I take anonymity very seriously, and I don't usually tell people I'm in recovery unless they're in recovery themselves, or if I think it's important that they know. For example, I told my current girlfriend on our first date, but I had known her for a couple months before that and I thought she could keep it in confidence. I've also told prospective employers, if they asked about holes in my resume or something like that. I tell them that I was addicted to video games, that I ruined my life by playing too much, and that I haven't played for the past four years. People are usually pretty satisfied with that answer.

As I mentioned above, I am in a twelve-step fellowship for substance abusers, not digital addicts. I justify my participation in such a fellowship by the 3rd Tradition, and I maintain sobriety from substances partly out of respect for this tradition. My sponsor and most of my close friends know about the details of my situation, but I don't feel the need to explain myself to most of the people I come across in that program. I usually wait until I've known someone for about two or three months before having The Talk with them, and I wait until I'm fairly sure that they will be understanding. It doesn't really require any active deception on my part, I just don't bring it up and nobody really thinks to ask. If anyone does ask about my 'drug of choice', I just say that I liked using Adderall and playing video games and now I don't do either of those things. Nobody really asks that, not since I got out of re- hab. After three years of sobriety, I don't really think about video games much, so it doesn't come up very often. When I share at meetings, I talk about my recovery and the things going on in my day to day life, and make vague references to 'my active addic- tion' if I have to talk about it at all. I do this mainly out of a desire not to offend the old-timers, some of whom get bent out of shape if other addictions come up, but I also feel that keeping my story generic makes it a little more relatable. If something happens that I do need to talk about, like getting directly triggered or tempted by something, or abusing the internet to the point where I need to rethink my boundaries, I talk to my sponsor or the people in my network who know my situation.

Whether it's somebody in recovery or not, the responses I get are all across the map. A lot of the time people are curious and want to know more, occasionally I get someone who's com- pletely baffled and doesn't understand at all, but many times I've been surprised by people simply accepting it without question. I suspect many people who play video games or binge-watch TV shows know how easy it is to overdo electronic media, so the idea of a full-fledged digital addict isn't that strange. I've struggled with feeling like I don't fit in for a long time because of these issues, so finding someone who is accepting, even if they themselves can't fully understand what I go through, is extremely helpful.

Q: **Are you aware that there is a fellowship called Computer Gaming Addicts Anonymous? Have you ever been to a meeting online or in person? Were they helpful?**

A: I am aware of this fellowship, but I no longer attend their meetings. I haven't lived close enough to any of their face to face meetings to attend one, and I found their online meetings unhelpful. I attended several chat room meetings, but spending time watching a screen, just waiting for people to type a response, was extremely tempting for me. Ultimately, I decided it was doing my recovery more harm than good. They also have voice chat meetings, which I was never able to try. Maybe those would have been more helpful, but I still feel like the human contact that I feel in face to face meetings is very important to my recovery, and I don't think I could ever stay sober only using online meetings.

I did meet a number of people during my time in CGAA, and I still communicate with them over the phone. Unfortunately, they are all too far distant from me to see any of them face to face, but I still find conversing with them over the phone valuable because they understand my issues on such a deep, visceral level. I have even tried sponsoring people over the phone in the past, but they relapsed before we completed the steps. In any case, I find in person sponsorship more effective, but this addiction is so isolating by its very nature that it can be hard to find people who want the help.

Q: **If a parent is worried about their teenager's video game or social media use, what kind of questions should they ask or what behaviors should they look for?**

A: I've never been a parent, so it's difficult for me to speak from a parent's perspective. It's also difficult to draw the line between heavy use and abuse, when everybody has a smartphone and binge-watching Netflix is close to the national pastime. However, I think the two biggest signs for an addict of any age is using electronics for longer than they intend to, and getting online even when it's not their intention.

An example of the first one from my life is that I was supposed to hang out with a girl when I was in high school. I liked her a lot, and was really looking forward to seeing her. The day I was supposed to see her, I started playing a game and didn't stop until an hour after I was supposed to meet her in town. I legitimately wanted to see her, but that desire was secondary to the game.

An example of the second is when my parents finally convinced me that playing a certain game was hurting my grades, so I agreed to only play it on the weekends. I asked them to hide it somewhere I couldn't find it during the week so I wouldn't be tempted, legitimately wanting to avoid playing. Nevertheless, the next week I ransacked their room looking for it, and played until I got caught, even knowing I was going to get caught. I didn't want to start, but I found myself starting anyway. Another example is that often I had a project in a class due the next day that I was capable of finishing and truly wanted to finish, but played video games until I no longer had time to finish the project. I had no desire to spend any time online, but I did anyway; that is the clearest possible sign of addict behavior.

Q: **What message would you like to pass on to other people who might have internet gaming disorder?**

A: I would like to let them know that recovery from electronic addiction is possible, no matter how hopeless it may seem at this moment. When I was beginning my journey of recovery, I felt like it was impossible to give up my addiction and still lead a good life, because at the time electronics were the only thing that made me happy. Although I live my life very differently than most kids my age, my life is better than it ever was before in so many ways, and if I can do it, so can someone else. Recovery is possible, and having lived in both ways, I firmly believe recovery is worth it.

Recommendations

This chapter provides recommendations for various parties who may come into contact with individuals struggling with internet gaming disorder. Some of the suggestions are preventive and seek to decrease the development of new cases of internet gaming disorder. Other proposals are focused on treatment. We offer micro level advice on the relationship between parents and their children. Significant direction is focused on the macro level for the development of legislation and further research. Progress can only be made by taking a multifaceted approach.

Recommendations for Parents

Parents are essential in the public health effort to decrease the prevalence of Internet Gaming Disorder among children and teenagers. One of the first things parents can do is establish rules about video game use. A recent survey found that two-thirds of children live in households that have no rules regarding time spent with electronics. While the direct correlation between time playing video games and developing Internet Gaming Disorder is still being researched, it appears that greater time playing predisposes players to developing an addiction. Recent studies show that middle schoolers in the U.S. spend an average of four ½ hours per day consuming media on screen in the form of television, video games, cellphones, and using the internet. Boys spend much of their screen time playing video games while girls are more likely to use social media. We suggest parents should limit entertainment screen time to two hours per day. The two hours is only for time spent using screens for entertainment purposes and does not include time spent online for research, studying and homework (which should be monitored).

About 70% of children in the U.S. have a television in their bedroom. Up to 76% of children take an internet connected device to bed with them (the same report found that only 23% of parents monitor device usage). This can greatly impact sleep. Parents should keep televisions and internet connected devices out of the bedroom. This practice further strengthens limits by restricting access. Another suggestion is for parents to model appropriate video game behavior. It is hypocritical for them to place limits on their children's video game play when they are playing *Candy Crush* or *Angry Birds* at every free moment. Parents need to demonstrate and conform to healthy screen and video game habits.

Recommendations for Educators

A startling piece was published in the *New York Times* on October 26, 2018 titled "A Dark Consensus About Screens and Kids Begins To Emerge in Silicon Valley." A lot of the creators of the ubiquitous tech of the 21st century and executives from Apple, Microsoft, Google, Facebook and other Silicon Valley companies have exhibited alarm about the effects of screens and tech on their children, epitomized by this quote:

> *Athena Chavarria, who worked as an executive assistant at Facebook and is now at Mark Zuckerberg's philanthropic arm, the Chan Zuckerberg Initiative, said: "I am convinced the devil lives in our phones and is wreaking havoc on our children.*

The article lists famous executives and their rules regarding cell phones, video games, social media, and iPad use. Most are quite strict. Perhaps most significantly, many of these wealthy visionaries send their children to low-tech or no-tech school, ensuring that they are exposed to the (soon-to-be) luxury of human interaction and education.

After their homes, schools are the place children spend the greatest amount of their time. Schools can play a pivotal role in the prevention of and treatment of Internet Gaming Disorder. One of first actions schools should take is to include Internet Gaming Disorder in the health curriculum, starting in pre-school and being discussed every year through high school. Administrators, faculty, staff, and students need to be educated on what Internet Gaming Disorder is, risk factors for developing it, signs to look for in identifying it, and resources available for those afflicted. As Internet Gaming Disorder has been linked to poor academic performance, schools are the ideal institution to address this problem. Teachers should be alert for signs. Child study teams and school psychologists need to be trained in appropriate screening techniques and referral services. Administrators need to provide their faculty and staff with the requisite training and ensure that students and parents are properly informed.

It is increasingly common for schools to provide laptops or tables to students to use during the course of the school as well as for homework. Schools should partner with parents to provide education on appropriate time limit setting for using those devices. Additionally, schools should provide education and resources to parents to help in monitoring their children's use of those devices. Schools should also encourage parents to ensure that these internet connected devices stay out of their children's bedrooms.

Recommendations for Doctors

Doctors should follow the recommendations regarding media use from The American Academy of Pediatrics. Doctors should ask two media questions at every child's visit:

Is there a television or internet connected device in your
child's room?
How much recreational screen time does your child consume
on a daily basis?

These questions serve as an opportunity for doctors to evaluate
screen time and provide education to the parents about healthy
practices regarding screen use.

Doctors should also ensure that their staffs are educated on
Internet Gaming Disorder. Family practice medical professionals need to learn signs and symptoms, screening techniques,
and treatment options. This education can be provided to doctors, nurses, and physician assistants as part of their mandatory
continuing medical education (CME). Doctors can also provide
assistance and education regarding Internet Gaming Disorder to
schools and parent groups. They can leverage their position in the
community to advocate for greater education and empowerment
of parents in developing healthy video game rules.

Recommendations for Policy Makers

Federal policy makers should advocate for directing funds to
The National Institute of Health (NIH) to conduct the necessary
research on Internet Gaming Disorder. In 2010, the federal government awarded $3 million to the University of California-Irvine
to study the effects of playing *World of Warcraft* (WOW) and
developing friends. Unfortunately, the research was not focused
on the potential adverse side effects associated with video game
play. Studies are needed on the etiology of Internet Gaming Disorder, appropriate screening tools, efficacy of medication assisted
treatment, and the most effective therapeutic treatment modalities. The NIH is a part of the U.S. Department of Health and is the
largest biomedical research agency in the world. Without involv-

ing the NIH, the necessary research is likely to move forward at a glacial pace. Policy makers should remain abreast of the research on Internet Gaming Disorder. This will help them in shaping and designing appropriate legislation. The policies and legislation regarding video games in other countries should be studied. The Asia-Pacific Region is a good source of information, as many countries already have pertinent policies and legislation in place. Policy makers should be aware of treatment programs in other countries. By making themselves familiar with the practices and legislation in other countries, they can select and help implement the best practices.

Recommendations for Research

While there is enough evidence to support the existence of Internet Gaming Disorder, there are several areas that need to be examined more thoroughly. Research needs to be conducted to study the etiology of Internet Gaming Disorder. Etiology is simply the cause and progression of a disease. There have been a handful of studies on the progression of Internet Gaming Disorder, but they have produced mixed results. The studies found that anywhere from 26% to 84% of who were diagnosed addicted to video games were still in the throes of the problem two years later. That is a ridiculous range and additional research needs to be conducted to provide clarification. Once the cause and progression are understood, steps can be taken for better prevention techniques, as well as figuring out the most effective treatment modalities.

Further research needs to be orchestrated on the effectiveness of screening tools. There are many different screening measures that are used. However, research directed to ensure that these tools are valid and reliable is needed. Inaccurate screening tools lend themselves to underreporting or over-reporting the frequency of the disorder. They need to be reliable from person to person. Specific screening instruments may need to be designed for different age groups: a 10 year old is very different from a 17 year old or someone who is 26.

We need organized research to determine if there are certain video games or game designs whose players develop higher rates of addiction. It is hypothesized that massive multiplayer online role player games (MMORPGs) have player populations that have higher rates of Internet Gaming Disorder. Research needs to be conducted that helps determine if that is true. If there is a correlation, then additional research needs to be conducted to determine if there is causation. For example, researchers need to figure out if people who play *League of Legends* have higher rates of Internet Gaming Disorder or if people who have the disorder are more interested in playing it.

A handful of research has been done focusing on different therapeutic treatment modalities. Cognitive Behavioral Therapy (CBT) has been the most researched therapeutic modality for the treatment of Internet Gaming Disorder. 23 studies have been conducted examining the effectiveness of CBT in the treatment of Internet Gaming Disorder. They have shown some positive results (improvements in cognition and motivation), but it needs to be researched much more extensively. Another therapeutic modality that has been proposed is *Motivational Interviewing* (MI), which is a counseling method focused on fostering internal motivation for clients to change. MI has been proposed as a potential modality for treatment of Internet Gaming Disorder but there is a serious shortage of studies on its efficacy. Both CBT and MI are widely considered to be the most effective therapies for substance misuse and other process disorders.

Research needs to be conducted to examine the effectiveness of medication assisted treatment. A handful of studies have been examining the use of Bupropion in curbing cravings for playing video games. Bupropion is sold under the brand names Wellbutrin and Zyban, which are typically prescribed as an antidepressant and/or for smoking cessation. These studies produced mixed results: some showed Bupropion to be helpful in reducing cravings while others showed no significant effect.

Recommendations for Therapists

Parents, educators, and doctors may be tasked with identifying Internet Gaming Disorder, but therapists and clinicians will be the ones who actually treat it. Therapists and clinicians must remain abreast of new developments in the identification and treatment. As this disorder starts to become a topic of national discussion, therapists will start to see an influx of clients. Most will be referred by concerned parents and loved ones. Like doctors and educators, therapists have the opportunity to provide education to parents on Internet Gaming Disorder. They should obtain training on Internet Gaming Disorder as part of their continuing education units (CEUs)[1]. Resources and research on Internet Gaming Disorder are incredibly limited right now (hence this book).

---

1 We have already set up several trainings in 2019 for counselors, social workers and addiction treatment providers in the Northeast.

Moving Forward

While the ICD-11 provides a basic description of Internet Gaming Disorder, it still has to be fleshed out. I am hoping that the next iteration of the DSM will include video game addiction (I prefer this term, but I do not really care how it is labeled), and that it will be further developed, better explained, and contain very clear diagnostic criteria. Until it is included as a diagnosis in the DSM, neither the insurance companies nor Medicaid will pay for it. This means that only the upper middle class and above can currently afford it. Additionally, because there is no mechanism for third party payment, most professionals and companies lack the incentive to learn more about this, participate in research, or create programs to address it. Thus, it is extremely important that clinicians, researchers, policy makers, administrators and ordinary citizens advocate for the inclusion of video game addiction in the next DSM. This is our single strongest recommendation.

Unique Populations

During a presentation in the spring of 2019 near the Jersey Shore, a social worker who has a director level position at a nursing home stated that "video games have completely captivated the residents." She said that they have to cancel most of the activities both inside and outside of the home, because "residents are playing games on their phones or tablets or computers and won't leave their rooms." Andrew and I were shocked.

We had come across articles about how video games are good for old people, but we did not dive into them much (we were guilty of focusing at first on kids and young people and then later on working age adults). We decided to take a harder look. In December of 2017, a study out of the University of Montreal reported that "playing 3D-platform video games on a regular basis may improve cognitive functions in seniors and increase grey matter in the hippocampus." Only 33 seniors were in the study and "may improve" is an incredibly weak conclusion. We found other studies that stated that video games "slow the aging process" and can "improve memory." None of them really rung out with strong science (to discuss (and potentially debunk) them would require another chapter or book).

A 2016 study put out by the AARP and Entertainment Software Association (that's a curious team up) reported that 38% of adults over 50 play video games and that women (40%) outweigh men (35%). They claim that older gamers use computers (59%) more than mobile devices (57%) and that 40% of gamers play every day. While a majority said that they play to have fun, about a quarter of them said they play to "stay sharp."

NBC News ran a story on seniors and video games in August of 2019. One woman who was featured has logged over 3,500 hours on a game called *Animal Crossing*. "I don't have too much of a social life. I'm mostly stuck at home, and I don't know. It feels like company."

Seniors, particularly those in assisted living facilities or nursing homes, are more likely than non-seniors to live sedentary lifestyles. This could be due to a number of factors, including: being overweight or obese, sickness, injuries, security fear, nervousness about the weather, lack of companions, wanting to stay close to a toilet, or depression. When dealing with those conditions, it becomes obvious that it can be quite the task for geriatric social workers, para professionals, volunteers, and interns to get seniors to go outside, take a dance class, do yoga, work on puzzles, make crafts, or engage in some other recreational activity. Given some thought, we think that the senior population is ripe for developing video game addiction.

At another presentation, several social workers who specialize in treating children and adults with autism told us about how so many of their clients spend an inordinate amount of time playing video games and "absolutely freak out" when the games are taken away. "And let me tell you," one of the social workers said, "that we are used to freak outs and melt downs. And some of the worst ones we've ever dealt with are because their video game was taken away."

Neither Andrew nor I know much about the autism spectrum. We have very little experience teaching or counseling people on the spectrum, and the articles and studies we found on the subject of autism and video games are all over the place. Like the aforementioned seniors, this is a vulnerable population that has the potential to be hit hard by video game addiction. While we are happy to provide information and assist with spitballing ideas, discussing research, and consulting with therapists, we firmly believe that professionals that specialize in autism should be looking into this and leading the work. We advise parents of children to have very clear rules and consequences around video games, and to consider significantly limiting access.

Personal History

My sister had the *Atari 2600* in the early 80's. She kept it in her room and only allowed me to play it a few times. I remember really liking *Keystone Cops, Q*Bert,* and *Pitfall Harry.* I didn't develop a skill with any of the games because of the sharp time limit and semi-hostile environment. Even given more time with those games, I don't believe that I would have gotten hooked (Andrew wrote about how neither the graphics, game play, nor stories were engaging enough to hold players' attention back then). My grandmother gave me the *Nintendo Entertainment System (NES)* when I was 10 and I acquired a few dozen games over the next 18 months. Most were easily winnable and didn't require a great deal of time (*The Legend of Zelda* was an exception and the first one that inspired a craze in my middle school due to its engaging narrative). I was busy with school, soccer, violin, piano, walks in the woods and long bike rides. I liked playing Nintendo, but my parents, particularly my father, looked upon the games with disdain and while there were no official rules about time, the hours that I could devote to video games were limited.

When I was 12, my grandmother bought me the *Sega Genesis*. It was the first mass market 16-bit system (*NES* was 8-bit). Because the graphics, gameplay, and stories were far better, I spent more time playing the *Genesis* than I had the *NES*. Sleepovers with friends probably consisted of 25%-50% game playing, as we tried to win games that required teamwork (*Gauntlet*) or allowed for two vs. two battles (*General Chaos* and *Madden Football*). There was a strong social component. Video games didn't negatively impact my schoolwork, sports, time with friends or other leisure activities.

The next generation of gaming consoles came out in the mid-90's, with the *Sony Playstation* and *Sega Saturn*. Once again, there was a massive leap in graphics, gameplay, and stories. At this point, I was quite busy with college, the Army and work. When I arrived at Rutgers in the fall of 1997, I was horrified by a young man who lived in the next room—he would play a *Tekken* (a player vs. player fighting game) somewhere between 12 and 18 hours a day, every day. It began a running joke in our dorm. People would ask him why he played so much and his two standard answers were "It's a great fucking game!" and "There's nothing better to do." Because of this young man, I swore off video games completely for the next several years.

In 2001, I saw Electronic Art's *Madden Football* for *the Sony Playstation 2 (PS2* was a 6th generation console) at a friend's apartment. I was flabbergasted at the quality of the graphics. More so, I was entranced by the game's capabilities. Growing up, a single player could only play a single season (16 games plus playoffs) in football games. *Madden* for *PS2* allowed for multiple players to play multiple seasons, a feature called dynasty mode (multiple people playing in the same sports league, season after season). This allowed us to each control a team, play 16 games, draft players out of college, make trades, build stadiums, move franchises, alter uniforms and pour over hundreds of various ratings and statistics. For a nerdy sports buff with a similar peer group, it was a dream. I bought a *PS2*, recruited friends, and for the next dozen years five to twelve of us played a few seasons each fall. We would get together in person and play on most Friday nights for three to four months. While two people played against each other, the rest of us would talk, eat and laugh. It was incredibly social. More than half of our league was in long-term recovery from alcohol and/or drugs.

In 2005, a few people who were in early recovery (less than one year clean) joined the league. All did well socially and remained sober, though one young man had serious academic problems because he spent hours and hours every day practicing (this was my second experience with problematic gaming). In 2007, my group moved on to Xbox 360 (7th generation); once again, we had been collectively wowed by the improvement in graphics and gameplay. We joked that we would be playing together deep into our 50s. When I took a job at Rutgers in 2009 as a counselor and oversaw the recovery houses, I used the Madden league as a way to provide a welcoming and sober support group to new students in recovery. It was so successful I included it in an article for *Addiction Professional* in 2011 (a copy of the article can be found in the Appendix). We ordered huge amounts of sushi on Friday nights, took photos of each other in team apparel, teased, joked and had a the occasional bouts of serious conversations.

I grew up on console gaming and the original business model of a single purchase of a game cartridge. In 2012, I witnessed the transition to subscription gaming. That year, Electronic Arts did away with the traditional dynasty mode in *Madden*. The only way to play a dynasty with friends was for each of us to buy a *Xbox 360*, a copy of *Madden 2013*, and an online Xbox subscription for $59.99.

We couldn't believe it, and we searched online forums for other peoples' reactions. There were a number of groups who did what we did – gather around once every seven to fourteen days and play games while socializing. They expressed their frustration and indignation that the original model was no longer possible. I was stunned. "Why would they get rid of the mode that so many people like? We use it as a social tool. It's like they want us all to be Bowling Alone."

Andrew Cartine, a cynical friend of mine who often irritated others with his negative but spot on assessments of business, government and society, said, "They don't care about you. They lose money on us. Ten people sitting around one console and one game makes them no money. If seven of us quit but three people each buy a console, get the game, and purchase the online subscription, they've more than tripled their money."

"But everyone that plays is going to be sitting in rooms by themselves. It's terrible for people. This is woefully against society," I responded.

"I can't believe how naïve you are," Andrew retorted. "They will make more money this way. A lot more. You and people like you that stop playing is an acceptable business loss. They've already figured that out."

We teased Andrew for being negative and cynical. That fall, we set up four gaming consoles in my basement, strung up cords all across the floor to get online, paid for the online accounts for those league members that didn't have money, and continued to hang out a few times a month. We lasted only one season. The online league was too difficult to manage and we ran into a number of technical glitches. The subscription model killed our video game football league (do not fret, we ended up moving on to board games and we regularly get together three to four times a month). And with that, I gave up video games for good.

Bowling Alone

I uttered "Bowling Alone" five paragraphs earlier. It was in reference to the book by Robert Putnam that was published in 2000 (it was an expansion of his 1995 essay—clearly, he had been thinking about this for a long time). Putnam argued that human interactions and social capital in America had drastically declined from the 1950s to the turn of the millennium. The title is in reference to the change in how Americans bowl. Despite an increase in bowling as a whole, bowling league participation had plummeted in the last 50 years. Bowling leagues are not just about bowling, but very much about social interaction and community bonding. Now, more and more people are just bowling alone.

Putnam wrote that over the second half of the 20th century, participation or membership in labor unions, religious groups, fraternal clubs and military veterans' organizations declined. He argued that this drop was partially tied to the rise of independent electronic forms of entertainment (television, movie rentals). I believe that this decline has been accelerated by overscheduling and the growth of fear culture in the 21st century.

His book was written in 2000, before the advent of high speed internet, advanced video games, and smart phones. I'm quite sure that isolation has dramatically increased in the two decades since publication. We are social creatures. We do better around other people. We need to interact (we are far more likely to laugh around others than by ourselves). When I treat people with anxiety or depressions or suicidal ideation, I ask about their friends and hobbies. Then I inquire about how often they see those friends and engage in those hobbies. "Are you part of something greater than yourself?" is another favorite question of mine. I don't care if that something is a church, team, civic organization, political group, hiking club or some other collection of humans. The people who have meaningful relationships, regular hobbies and a sense of engagement and purpose are less likely to develop anxiety or depression or suicidal thoughts. But if they do, they are much more likely to recover.

The Stress Response

The regular season games against the computer in our Madden league were pretty ho-hum. Our head-to head match-ups against each other were fairly intense. You could easily see the physical signs of stress: sweating, tense posture, contorted faces and the occasional yell. During the playoffs, these stress responses were magnified. One guy's wife said, "I don't know why you guys even play. None of you look like you are having fun. I don't even like walking by the room when you are playing, because it just feels so tense."

We did have fun, but I can understand her point. Most of us admitted that losing was at least twice as upsetting as winning was rewarding though. Dr. Daniel Kahneman, a behavioral economist who won the 2002 Nobel Prize and was the subject of Michael Lewis's *The Undoing Project*, wrote about how humans feel the pain of losing more than the pleasure of winning. For problematic gamblers and video game addicts, this is known as *loss chasing*. It keeps players coming back and is a key feature that is exploited by both game designers and casinos.

One of my clients from last summer provided me with textbook examples of both the stress response and loss chasing. I learned about *Fortnite* from him. He told me about this new game that was a massive online battle arena (MOBA). He said that he liked to take part in fights that pitted 100 people against each other. He stated that if he got killed very early, it wasn't a big deal. But when he got to the top 50 and then the top 25, he could feel "my blood pressure rise." He reported that he would tense up, sweat, get super focused, and yell and curse. "When I'm one of the final five, I can feel my heart exploding in my chest. It's crazy intense."

He said that when he experienced those "oh so close" losses, he would try to get into another 100 person battle immediately. I asked him about the effect of feeling that stressed for a long period of time. "It's exhausting. I've only won in a 100 man battle once, but I've been in the top five 21 times. It takes me a long time to wind down. When I finally do, I crash hard."

A 2018 study titled "The Beneficial or Harmful Effects of Computer Game Stress on Cognitive Functions of Players" had a sample size of 80 and measured the cortisol levels in saliva samples and brain wave variations before and after playing four types of games: a puzzle game, fear game, excitement game, and a runner game. When participants played the puzzle game, their stress levels were reduced. The other three games all significantly elevated stress levels. The fear game induced the highest levels of stress, and the researchers wrote that the stress was mostly the result of the "sound effects and music" instead of the visuals or the activity.

The findings of the fear game seem to be backed up by a 2005 study, which examined the contribution of music to the physiological stress of playing video games. Researchers had people play with music and with silence. The researchers reported that the stress levels were much higher during the music scenario than during silence.

We need more and larger studies on the stress responses to video game playing. I believe that game designers are fully aware of the effects of music/sound effects on gamers, and use it as an additional tool to keep consumers engaged (hooked). This is also an area that would benefit from further research.

Summary

Here are some key points that we want you to take away from this book (hopefully you haven't just skipped everything else to get here).

1) Games are played across the age spectrum. There are almost as many gamers over 36 (43%) as are under that age.
2) Females (45%) make up almost half of all gamers.
3) In regards to points 1 and 2, the most problematic video gamers are still likely to be male and in their teens or twenties. But the trends are already pointing out that females and older individuals rates of addictive gaming are increasing.
4) 47% of households do not have any rules regarding video games for people under 18 (amount played, time of day, type of game)
5) This is a massive industry that generates revenue of more than $130 billion per year and has experienced exponential growth over the last decade.
6) It is clear that games have become *more* addictive, partly based on improved graphics and gameplay, but also because of the online component, never ending stories, and the calculated reward system that has been implemented in modern games.
7) We did not go in depth about any games (not even *Fortnite*, the current belle of the ball), because the shelf life

of even the most popular games is pretty short. If I were writing a book on substance abuse, I would spend a lot of time on alcohol, benzodiazepines, heroin, nicotine, cocaine and marijuana, because those are drugs that have been abused for generations. Learning about them is a good expenditure of your time. One does not need to have a deep knowledge of *Halo* or *World of Warcraft* or *Starcraft 2* or *League of Legends* to understand the problems and pathology of video game addiction. There will be a new game that comes along in 2020 or 2021 that people will obsess over, that generates billions in revenue and dominates headlines. But the underlying causes and problems will remain largely the same.

8) Most people are completely unaware of *loot boxes*. These are ubiquitous in video games now. They are a $30 billion a year industry (compared to $6 billion a year made through gambling at all of the Las Vegas casinos). We believe that loot boxes are priming young video game players for gambling, similar to the way that prescription painkillers primed two generations of Americans for heroin.

9) We are fully aware that many of the examples that we provided in this book are extreme. They are entertaining, memorable and help get our points across. They are more likely to make media reports (that is how Andrew found some of them). We don't want to create (or contribute to) the perception that video game addiction must be over-the-top or life threatening. If video games are causing problems in either school, at work, with relationships, health, finances, or legal (very rare), then that is enough for an evaluation.

10) Despite this current and every expanding problem, there is not nearly enough research. We are hoping that non-profits, university professors, and government organiza-

tions hear the clarion call and help the world realize and understand and treat this problem.

11) I must reiterate my point that I opened this chapter with. There is a dire lack of both treatment programs and clinicians that have even an elementary knowledge of video game addiction. Research will help. So will stories in the media. But until Medicaid and insurance pay for treatment, there will be little incentive for programs to open.

Plan

This is for clinicians and medical professionals.

1) Until there is more research and better guidance from the next editions of the DSM and ICD, video game addiction should be treated as a *process disorder*, similar to substance abuse and gambling.

2) Because of the way video games are currently designed and the presence of loot boxes, we strongly recommend taking a 20 to 30 hours course on gambling. Most American states have some kind of Center of Compulsive Gambling that receives state and federal funding and provides those trainings.

3) In point seven of the summary section, I explained why we did not detail the different games currently on the market. But it is important that clinicians have a basic understanding of the games that their clients are playing (remember how my little information about *World of Warcraft* helped me reach the client in the introduction). Ask your client questions about the game(s) they are playing. Find out what type of game it is, learn about the story (if there is one), and how one levels up. They almost certainly talk freely and at length with you about this. They will grow more comfortable with you, a very

important part of the client-therapist relationship.

4) As 47% of households don't have any rules for video games (or likely any screen time), helping parents/guardians set rules and limits is both excellent prevention work and treatment.

5) Remember that the recommended screen time for ages 0-2 is zero hours per day, 2-6 is one hour per day, and 6-18 is two hours per day. When we share those numbers with professionals we train or clients in groups, almost everyone balks. This is because screens have become so perpetually intertwined in our lives.

6) Family work is of utmost importance. It will be hard for a teenager to end their video game addiction if they have a parent who is constantly looking at their phone (it's an issue of poor role modeling and also a bit of hypocrisy, which makes teens wild). Family and household members are massively impactful on each other's lives. They can be a huge well of support or an incredible source of stress. I have had great success engaging in multi-family work in substance abuse treatment programs and believe that it can be similarly impactful in regards to gaming.

7) Video game detox works. Much like quitting alcohol or opioids or nicotine, the immediate aftermath of quitting is the hardest. There are less than five inpatient programs in America for video game addiction (and remember, they have no data). One may take a harm reduction approach and try to get their clients to cut down their hours. That may work in some cases, but it is more likely going to help illustrate the lack of control that your client is experiencing.

8) The role of community is significant. This was explained in the *Bowling Alone* section of this chapter. Clients should not quit video games and then just watch a lot of Netflix (or start vaping). Participation in clubs, sports, religious services and other activities involving face-to-

face contact is an essential (I argue that it is *the* essential) piece of the recovery process. Help your clients connect with others.

Conclusion

Internet Gaming Disorder is just starting to be discussed in the U.S. The American community overall is not educated or equipped to handle this growing public health problem. Parents should set limits on screen time (2 hours per day) and model proper behavior.

All parties need to work together collectively. Doctors and therapists need to become educated so that they can share their knowledge with parents and empower them. Doctors, educators, parents, and clinicians need to advocate to policy makers about the importance of developing legislation regarding video games and the treatment of Internet Gaming Disorder. Policy makers need to provide funding for further research. Researchers need to fill in the knowledge gaps regarding video game addiction.

Despite Andrew's research on this topic and Frank's experience counseling a few dozen clients over the years, there is much that we don't know. We opened up a treatment program in Morris County, New Jersey to treat this rapidly growing disorder in the spring of 2019. We plan on bringing in researchers from a variety of universities and expect to conduct a series of clinical trials involving different counseling methods, technologies, and medications. We expect that we will look back at this book and say "we really got that part wrong" and hope we can point to a few sections that we got right.

Without a doubt, the second edition will be better. This is where you come in. If you read about new research, let us know. If you hear about a policy or law that improves prevention, drop us an email. If you are a therapist and think you have effective counseling strategies, call us immediately. It is going to take a community effort.

Appendices

Building a campus recovery community

Frank L. Greenagel Jr., LCSW, LCADC, ACSW, CJC

Rutgers University was founded in 1766 and became the state university of New Jersey in 1945. In 1972, Rutgers College, the premier college within the university, became a co-ed institution. The school's Alcohol and Drug Assistance Program (ADAP) was created in 1983. Lisa Laitman, MSED, LCADC, was hired to educate and counsel students on Rutgers' Newark, New Brunswick and Camden campuses about substance abuse. Her first boss wondered if Laitman "would have enough work to do."

In 1988, Laitman created Recovery Housing on the New Brunswick campus, the first on-campus housing in the U.S. for students in recovery from alcohol and drug dependence. In 1993, Recovery Housing opened on the Newark campus. There are 25 beds in New Brunswick (which has its own on-campus house) and eight in Newark (in two apartments in a dorm). Resident students must be sober at least 90 days, have a sponsor and attend at least two 12-Step meetings a week. To get in, students must apply to Rutgers for admission and must contact the ADAP staff and set up an interview.

More than 350 students have resided in the specialized housing. Students have ranged in age from 17 to 43, but typically fall between 18 and 26. Undergraduates, master's candidates, law students and PhD candidates have lived there. In 2008, ADAP held its 25th-year reunion, attended by more than 125 alumni.

I was hired at Rutgers in the spring of 2009 under a grant from New Jersey's Division of Addiction Services. I was tasked to help recovering students access university resources, provide academic counseling, improve students' connection with the local recovery community, develop activities for students to have fun, and reduce the stigma that some experienced in being in recovery on a college campus. My first move was to reach out to the 60-plus ADAP alumni who still lived within 30 minutes of Rutgers, to ask what changes needed to be made and if they would be willing to serve as mentors and sponsors.

The alumni response was tremendous. They pointed out what worked (the existence of the house, the individual counseling at ADAP, the activities at Rutgers) and what didn't (there should be at least a 90-day waiting period before moving in, some students don't go to meetings for a week or two at a time, there is a need for quicker interventions by staff when a student's behavior seems strange). Many of the alumni's suggestions were implemented.

In August 2009, 23 students (11 returned from the previous year) and 13 alumni attended a move-in orientation at the Recovery House in New Brunswick. Students introduced themselves, and the alumni talked about their sobriety date, major, when they lived in the Recovery House, their year of graduation, what they do now, and their strongest piece of advice to students about living in the house and/or attending college (don't date anyone in the house, don't let the Recovery House be your only source of support, attend all of your classes, write for the school newspaper, study abroad). Next, students had to fill out a form that matched a particular life experience to a particular alumnus (who has run a marathon, who has never smoked a cigarette). Afterwards, a barbeque provided a more laid-back atmosphere for students and alumni to converse.

In August 2010, 23 students were joined by 16 alumni for orientation. After the introductions and advice by the alumni, an AA meeting was held in the house (another eight members of the recovery community showed up for that). The barbeque lasted deep into the night.

This article first appeared in the March 2011 issue of *Addiction Professional*, an online journal. https://psychcongress.com/article/building-campus-recovery-community

Current Analysis of the Gaming Industry

The gaming industry has experienced spectacular growth. Viewing services like Twitch have become mainstream. It is normal to see live gaming on ESPN. Tens of thousands of fans routinely fill venues to watch gaming competitions. While the general public may know that the gaming industry is doing well, very few know the extent. The gaming industry has experienced yearly double-digit growth for almost a decade straight.[1] The industry is expected to generate $138 billion in worldwide revenue in 2018.[2] By 2022, revenue is projected to be somewhere between $180 million to $230 billion.[3] [4] The gaming industry has exploded. A look to the past helps shed light on why.

The gaming industry traces its roots to arcade games like Atari's *Pong* and Magnavox's home game console the Odyssey. The initial growth in the gaming industry occurred as consoles became popular and arcades entered a golden age. In 1981 the industry generated $5 billion in revenue.[5] It suddenly collapsed in 1983. The North American home console market experienced decreases in sales from $3.2 billion in 1982 to $100 million in

---

1   https://newzoo.com/insights/articles/global-games-market-reaches-137-9-billion-in-2018-mobile-games-take-half/
2   https://www.cnbc.com/2018/07/18/video-game-industry-is-booming-with-continued-revenue.html
3   https://www.marketwatch.com/press-release/digital-gaming-market-will-grow-18000-billion-by-2022-2018-05-28
4   https://www.digi-capital.com/news/2018/01/games-software-hardware-165b-in-2018-230b-in-5-years-record-2b-investment-last-year/#.WI6JKKinGUm
5   https://books.google.com/books?id=XiMOntMybNwC&pg=PA105#v=onepage&q&f=false

1985.[6] Many predicted it would not survive. Buoyed by Japanese game consoles, the industry emerged from the crash in the late 80's. For next two decades, Japan was the industry leader. The industry experienced slow and steady growth. In 2007, 35 years after the start of the gaming industry as it is known, revenues finally exceeded $35 billion.[7]

It took the gaming industry 35 years to generate $35 billion in revenue. In the following eleven years, it added another $100 billion per year. How did the industry triple yearly revenue in a third of the time? The iPhone was released in 2007.[8] It ushered in the age of the smart phone, and modern mobile gaming. Sales in the mobile gaming sector have grown exponentially every year.

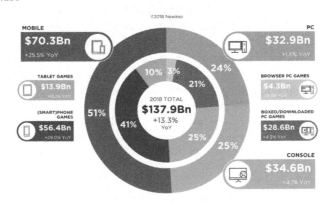

2018 GLOBAL GAMES MARKET
PER DEVICE & SEGMENT WITH YEAR-ON-YEAR GROWTH RATES

©2018 Newzoo

MOBILE

$70.3Bn
+25.5% YoY

PC

$32.9Bn
+1.6% YoY

TABLET GAMES
$13.9Bn
+13.2% YoY

BROWSER PC GAMES
$4.3Bn
+13.9% YoY

(SMART)PHONE GAMES
$56.4Bn
+29.0% YoY

BOXED/DOWNLOADED PC GAMES
$28.6Bn
+4.5% YoY

2018 TOTAL
$137.9Bn
+13.3% YoY

10% 3% 24% 21% 51% 41% 25% 25%

CONSOLE
$34.6Bn
+4.1% YoY

Source: ©Newzoo | 2018 Global Games Market Report
newzoo.com/globalgamesreport

6 https://www.uh.edu/engines/epi3038.htm
7 https://arstechnica.com/gaming/2008/06/gaming-expected-to-be-a-68-billion-business-by-2012/
8 https://www.fiercewireless.com/wireless/timeline-apple-iphone-rumors-1999-present

In 2018, the mobile gaming sector has become the biggest force in the gaming industry.[9] The chart below illustrates the various sectors of the video game industry and their respective revenue projections for 2018.

The mobile gaming sector is projected to generate $70.3 billion in worldwide revenue in 2018. This represents more than 50% of total revenue generated in the gaming industry. Further illustrating the popularity of smartphones as devices for mobile gaming, the bottom left of the chart shows smartphones are projected to generate $56.4 billion, or 80% of the mobile revenue. In 2018, mobile gaming is projected to generate $20 billion more in revenue than the entire gaming industry generated in 2007. In just 11 years, mobile gaming has gone from being the smallest sector in the gaming industry to the largest one. The console and PC sectors are still healthy and produce significant returns, representing 25% and 24% of the gaming industry revenues respectively.

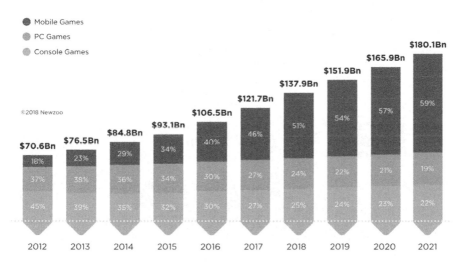

The chart above is a combination of revenue generated to date by each sector in the gaming industry as well as their respective projections through 2021. The chart illustrates the explosive growth of mobile gaming at 5-6% each year. A quick glance would give the impression that the mobile market has cut into the revenue from PCs and consoles. After all, the PC share decreased from 37% in 2012 to 24% in 2018 and the console share decreased from 45% to 25%. Mobile games are not cutting into the PC or console markets. The mobile game sector is simply growing faster.

Between 2012 and 2018, the console sector revenue increased from $31.8 billion to $34.4 billion, an 8% growth in revenue. PC revenue increased from $26.1 billion to $33.09 billion in 2018. This represents a 26.9% increase. The revenue growth for PC gaming and console gaming is healthy. However, between 2012 and 2018 mobile gaming revenue increased from $12.7 billion to $70.3 billion, a growth of 450%. Revenue is expected to increase gradually for PC games and consoles in years to come, with the majority of the growth in the gaming industry occurring in the mobile sector.

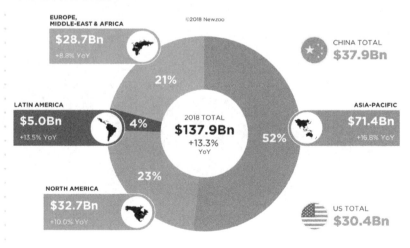

Source: ©Newzoo | April 2018 Quarterly Update | Global Games Market Report
newzoo.com/globalgamesreport

Global Analysis

On the global scale, the Asia-Pacific region is projected to generate the most revenue in 2018 ($71.4 billion). This represents 52% of worldwide revenue. The Asia-Pacific region has the largest consumers of video games in China and the most mature market in Japan. The Chinese market is projected to generate $37.9 billion. The Japanese market is projected to generate $19.2 billion in revenue in 2018. Revenues in the Asia-Pacific region are projected to increase by 16.8% which is predominately due to increases in the mobile game sector. With India's large population and the emergence of Southeast Asian, in particular Thailand, the Asia-Pacific region will continue to be a force in the gaming industry worldwide for years to come.

The North American industry is projected to experience a 10% increase from 2017 to 2018. Sales in North America region are led by the United States (projected to be $30.4 billion in 2018). The United States has the largest number of employees in the gaming industry with 140,000 employees who work directly or indirectly in the industry. The average salary for those who work directly in the gaming industry is $94,000.[10] These high salaries help draw talent who thereby produce quality products for domestic distribution which drive the industry in the North America region. The United States is also home to game developers such as Activision Blizzard, Electronic Arts, and Take-Two Interactive. All three are market leaders in the world.[11] [12] [13]

Europe, Middle East, and Africa is the third largest region in the video game industry. Growth in this region has been slow due to lower levels of smartphone ownership in Africa. As mobile gaming is the fastest growing sector in the gaming industry, lack of access to smartphones has slowed growth in this region.

10 http://www.theesa.com/article/u-s-video-game-industrys-economic-impact/
11   https://www.activision.com/company/locations/santa-monica
12 https://corporateofficehq.com/electronic-arts-corporate-office/
13 https://www.reuters.com/finance/stocks/company-profile/TTWO.O

Glossary

Action game: a game genre that emphasizes physical challenges. It includes fighting games and shooters

Action role-playing game (ARPG): a genre of role-playing video game where battle actions are performed in real-time

Adventure game: a game genre which emphasizes exploration and puzzle-solving

Arcade game: a coin-operated game machine. Popular primarily during the 70s-80s. Note arcade games are still very popular in Japan

Auto-aim (also known as aim-assist): a game mechanic built into the game to make it easier to lock onto targets for faster aiming

Avatar: the player's representation in the game world

Badge: an indicator of accomplishment, skill, or work showing that a player has performed some particular action within the game

Battle pass: an in-game purchase which unlocks additional content that is not available in the free version of games

Battle royale game: a video game genre that is focused on last-man standing. Players search for equipment while attempting to eliminate their opponents

Boosting: when a player with a low-ranked level has a more skilled player use their account to improve their character level. There is an entire industry focused on providing this service to players who are willing to pay

Bot: short for robot. A non-playable character in the game which is controlled by artificial intelligence

Campaign mode: a series of levels in a game intended to tell a story

Camping: a strategy in which a player stays in one place (typically a fortified position) for an extended period of time and waits to ambush opponents. This is a typical strategy in first-person shooter games

Capture the flag: a multiplayer game mode in which the goal is to capture the flag of the opposing team while simultaneously defending your own flag

Casual gaming: playing video games on an infrequent basis

Challenge mode: a game mode beyond normal play in which the conditions are much more difficult

Character class: most common in role-playing games. Characters are jobs or professions that come with a predetermined series of attributes and skills

Cheat: a game code that allows players to beat the game or gain a significant advantage over their opponents

Checkpoint: an area in the game level from which players will start the next time that they day. Instead of reverting back all the way to the beginning when they die players go back to their most recent checkpoint

Combo: a series of attack strung together to increase the damage done to opponents

Compulsion loop: a design in gameplay which is a continuous cycle. This encourages players to play for longer periods of time through the use of rewards

Console: a video game hardware unit that typically connects controllers to a screen. Popular consoles include Xbox, Playstation, and the Nintendo Switch

Console Wars: refers to the battle between Sega and Nintendo in the 80s and 90s

Content rating: classifying system for video games which determines which age the game is appropriate for. Similar to the ratings of movies

Cooldown: the minimum length of time that the players needs to wait after using an ability before they can use it again. Think of it as the amount of time you need to wait before touching a pan that has been in the oven

Cooperative gameplay (co-op): multiplayer game mode in which players compete together to fight computer-controlled opponents

Crafting: a game element in which players can design their own armor, weapons, or medicines. Very common in massive multiplayer online games

Deathmatch (free-for-all): a game mode in many shooter and real-time strategy games in which the objective is to kill as many other characters as possible until a time limit or kill limit is reached. For example *Call of Duty* has a deathmatch option in which teams compete against each other in a race to reach 75 total kills

Developer: the production company which designs and makes the video game

Downloadable content: additional content for a video game which can be downloaded remotely

Drop rate: the probability of obtaining an item from a loot box

Electronic sports: organized competitions in which teams compete against each other while audiences can watch in-person of via streaming services. *eSports*

Experience point: experience points are used to illustrate progress towards the next character level

Farming: repeating a battle, quest, or other part of the game in order to receive in-game currency or rewards. Gold farming is the most prominent example

First-person shooter (FPS): a genre of video game where the player experiences the game from the first-person perspective and the primary purpose is to use guns to defeat the enemy

Frag: to injure or kill an opponent with a grenade

Freemium: the pricing strategy in which games are free to play with the option for players to make in-game purchases. The most common strategy used today by video game design companies

God mode: a cheat in which players become invincible.

Grinding: performing a repetitive and time-consuming action in a video game before being able to advance

Handheld console: a portable game console. For example the Nintendo Gameboy

Health: the number showing how much damage a character can take before being killed

Influencer: a video game player or social media personality paid to be part of a game's promotion

Inventory: a menu or area of the screen where items collected by the player-character during the game can be selected

Kill-death ratio: a statistic that compares the number of times a player kills opponents vs. the number of times they die. A high kill-death ratio indicates that a player is skilled

Lag: a delay between player input and corresponding action in the game

Last man standing: a multiplayer deathmatch mode in which the objective is to be the last person alive

Level: a location in the game or the experience level of a player in a role-playing game (RPG). The higher the level a player has in a RPG the more skilled they are

Localization: the process of editing a game during publishing to ensure the game is appropriate for different areas. Belgium has outlawed loot boxes. Instead of creating a new game without loot boxes game publishers could just remove them from games in Belgium to remain in accordance with the law

Loot box: awarded to players for completing a match, gaining experience level, or through direct purchases. Loot boxes contain random items. Loot boxes generated over $30 billion in revenue for game companies in 2018 alone

Massive multiplayer online game (MMO): a game that involves a large community of players in a virtual world

Massive multiplayer online role-playing game (MMORPG): a MMO that includes role-playing game mechanics. *World of Warcraft* is the most well-known MMORPG

Microtransaction: a business model in which players can make in-game purchases

Multiplayer online battle arena (MOBA): a genre which pits teams of players to defend their home base from enemy onslaughts. *Defense of the Ancients* is a very popular MOBA game

Multiplayer: a game that allows multiple players to play at the same time

Non-player character (NPC): a character that is not controlled by a player

Online game: a game that can be player online. Most multiplayer games support online play

Power-up: an object that temporarily gives the player a boost in health or ability

Publisher: the company that finances, distributes, and markets the game

Quest: an activity designed in a game for either story of character development. *World of Warcraft* has quests that players can go on to improve their skill and get prizes

Raid: a type of mission in a game where a group of players attempt to defeat another team or computer controlled opponents

Respawn: the reappearance of a character or enemy after their death

Role-playing game: a game in which the player takes on the role of a specific character and acquires new skills and abilities as they advance through the game

Skin: a customization option for a player's in-game avatar. Very popular currently in *Fortnite*

Unlock: gaining access to game content by advancing through the game or reaching certain achievement levels

https://en.wikipedia.org/wiki/Glossary_of_video_game_terms

Bibliography

United States

Gentile, D. (2009). Pathological video-game use among youth ages 8 to 18. *Psychological Science 20*(5). – article detailing study on video game addiction prevalence in the United States.

Choo, H., Gentile, D., Sim, T., Li, D., Khoo, A., & Liau, A. (2010). Pathological video-gaming among Singaporean youth. *Annals Academic of Medicine 39.* 822-829. Article discusses prevalence of video game addiction among Singaporean youth and youth from other regions of the world.

Neuroscience

Zastrow, M. (2017). Is video game addiction really an addiction? *Proceedings of the National Academy of Science of the United States of America. 114*(17). 4268-4272 – study discussing how video game addiction is gaining traction as a real disorder in the U.S. Discusses studies that have explored the neurological impact of sustained video game play. Finally compares brain imagining results for those addicted to video games to other traditional addictions.

Pan, N., Yang, Y., Du, X., Qi, X., Du, G., Zhang, Y., Li, X., & Zhang, Q. (2018). Brain structures associated with internet addiction tendency in adolescent online game players. *Front Psychiatry 6*(9). – article discussing studies exploring the neurological impact of video game addiction.

Weng., C., Qian, R., Fu, X., Lin, B., Han, X., Niu, C., & Wang, Y. (2013). Gray matter and white matter abnormalities in online game addiction. *European Journal of Radiology 82*(8). 1308-1312. – article discusses the reduction of gray and white matter in different regions of the brain for video game addicts

History

Harris, B. (2015). Console Wars: Sega, Nintendo, and the Battle that Defined a Generation. New York, NY. HarperCollins Publishers.

Kent, S. (2001). The Ultimate History of Video Games: From Pong to Pokemon – The Story Behind the Craze that Touched Our Lives and Changed the World. New York, NY. Three Rivers Press – book on the history of the video game industry up until the start of the 21st century.

Desjardins, J. (2017) How video games became a $100 billion industry. *Visual Capitalist* – long article covering the history of the video game industry. Includes an exceptional graphic map showing the major events which shaped the industry over its entire existence.

Chikhani, R. (2015). The history of gaming: an evolving community. *Techcrunch* – article that discusses the history of gaming in exact detail.

Asia

Robinson, M. (2015). Korea's internet addiction crisis is getting worse, as teens spend up to 88 hours a week gaming. Business Insider Australia. – This article provides an in-depth look at video game addiction in South Korea

(2019). Survey data, case studies suggest gaming addiction rampant among Japan's youth. The Mainichi. – Article on how Japan is experiencing a significant problem with video game addiction among its youth.

Saunders, J., Hao, W., Long, J., King, D., Mann, K., Fauth,Buhler,

M. et. Al. (2017) Gaming disorder: Its delineation as an important condition for diagnosis, management, and prevention. *Journal of Behavior Addictions* 6(3). 271-279. – Study of video game addiction which discusses prevalence rates in Asian countries as well as European countries.

Huhh, J. (2007). PC bang Inc.: The Culture and Business of PC Bangs in Korea. *SSRN Electronic Journal*. – Article discusses PC bangs and the role they play in South Korean Culture.

Board, J. (2019). End game: The rise of esport empires in Thailand and their armies of addicts. Channelnewsasia. – Article that discusses the popularity of esports in Thailand and video game addiction.

Apisitwasana, N., Perngparn, U., & Cottler, L. (2017). Gaming addiction situation among elementary school students in Bangkok, Thailand. *Indian Journal of Public Health Research and Development* 8(2). – Article that discusses the rising prevalence of video game addiction among Thai youth.

Li, W. (2018). Eighteen percent of Chinese teens are at risk of video game addiction, says report. GB Times. – An article that discusses how up to 18% of Chinese youth are at risk for video game addiction.

General

Hsu, T. (2018). Video game addiction tries to move from basement to doctor's office. The New York Times. – This article was published after the World Health Organization (WHO) officially recognized Internet Gaming Disorder as a real diagnosis.

D'Anastasio, C. (2015). How video game addiction can destroy your life. Vice – an article that provides real-life examples of the depths that video game addiction can take people to.

Prescott, A. T., Sargent, J. D., & Hull, J. G. (2018). Metaanalysis of the relationship between violent video game play and physical aggression over time. *Proceedings of the National Academy of Sciences of the United States of America. 115*(40). 9882-9888. – Journal article on Dartmouth study which links playing violent video games to heightened levels of aggression.

Zendle, D., Meyer, R., & Over, H. (2019). Adolescents and loot boxes: links with problem gambling and motivations for purchase. *The Royal Society.* – A study on the link between loot boxes and gambling from the U.K. Gambling addiction among youth quadrupled in a two year period and this study explores the role loot boxes played in the increase.

Zendle, D., & Cairns, P. (2019). Loot boxes are again linked to problem gaming: Results of a replication study. *PloS ONE 14*(3). – Replication study which explores the link between loot boxes and gambling addiction.

Freed, R. (2018). The Tech Industry's War on Kids: How Psychology is being Used as a Weapon Against Children. Medium. – An article that provides an in-depth look at how psychology is used by technology companies and video game design companies. Includes a look at the work of B.J. Fogg

Perez, D. (2018). Skinner's Box and Video Games: How to Create Addictive Games. LevelSkip. – Article that discusses how the work of B.F. Skinner can be adopted to make loot boxes more addictive.

Movies:

Junge, D. (2019). Game Changers: Inside the Video Game Wars. – 2 hour special on The History Channel which covers the first 50 years of the video game industry in-depth. This is an exceptional movie.

(2018). Inside America's First Video Game Rehab. HBO. – Documentary that gives an inside look into ReStart, the first residential treatment program in the United States for video game addiction.

(2014). China's Web Junkies: Internet Addiction Documentary. The New York Times – A short documentary on video game addiction in China and their treatment at military boot camps.

Index

A

Addicted and Non-addicted Players 91
addiction camps 56
addictiveness of *World of Warcraft* 75
American Medical Association 86
Angry Birds 24
augmenting the progression 74

B

Bowling Alone 126
building rapport 80
Bupropion 120
business model of gaming industry 36

C

Candy Crush 25
casinos 71
character advancement 76
computer cafes 42
confusing exchange rates 74
current analysis of the industry 139

D

death matches 22
digital detox 46
DOTA 2 international world championship 28
DSM 5 criteria 87
dynasty mode 124

E

educators 116
endowed progress 78
eSports 27, 44, 49
etiology of Internet Gaming Disorder 119

F

fake currency 74
FarmVille 69
Fogg, B.J. 66
Fortnite 25, 78
Fortnite world cup 78
freemium 38, 65

G

Game Addiction in the U.S. 32
gamers 27
gaming among women 29
gaming industry 139
gaming industry revenue 27
Gentile, Douglas 32, 83, 85
gold farming 51, 77

H

health curriculum 117
history of gaming 14

I

ICD-11 87
International Classification of Disease 49
internet fasting camps 48
Internet Gaming Disorder) 7

L

loot boxes 71,130
loss chasing 127

M

manipulative psychology 65
massively multiplayer online role player games 43,120
massive online battle arena 128
micro transactions 38
MMORPG 24
motivational interviewing 120
multiplayer gaming 15
multiplayer online battle arena 24

P

parents 115
pathological gaming tendencies 33
PC Bangs 42
Pong 15, 40
process disorder 131
professional gaming 44
professional gaming industry 23
Putnam, Robert 126

R

random drops 77
recognizing addiction 80
recommendations 115
  recommendations for doctors 117
  recommendations for policy makers 118
  recommendations for research 119
  recommendations for therapists 121
  recommended screen time 132
rules about video game use 115

S

screening 82
Shutdown Law 46
Skinner, B.F. 68

Stanford Behavior Design Lab 66
StarCraft 43

T

treatment facilities 49
treatment programs 35
Twitch 139

U

User Research Lead 67

V

video game addiction 7
Video Game Addiction in Asia 40
    China 51
    Japan 47
    South Korea 40
    Thailand 60

W

World of Warcraft 75

Acknowledgements

Andrew's acknowledgements: I want to start by thanking Kaitlin Vanderhoff. From early on in the process Kaitlin was supportive and provided relentless encouragement. Without her stubborn support this book would not have been possible. Next I want to thank Frank Greenagel, my editor. This book would not have been possible without your constant pressure to expand my belief of what was possible. Finally, I want to thank my family. At various points throughout the writing process I was burnt out and had little emotional energy for interaction with my family. Thank you for understanding and being supportive.

Frank's acknowledgements: I would like to thank Arielle Cardone for her wonderful artwork that appears on the cover (and apologize to my niblings for not using the photo of them playing video games). I think that Matt's story provides real depth to the book, and I am so grateful to him for the time and energy he put in to meeting with me, answering questions and all of his written responses. Shayla Carroll performed much needed copy editing on several of the chapters. Andrew did the bulk of the research here and took the editorial suggestions without getting upset. He was also quite patient about the various delays. I told him this summer that he can do all of the presentations without me, which is evidence of my high level of trust and respect. This book doesn't exist without my father, who served as the final editor. He designed the book, chose the type, layout and was wonderful in offering up everything that he learned in publishing and writing over his 50+ year career. I have been so fortunate.

Screening for Video Game Addiction

1. Over time, have you been spending much more time playing video games, learning about video game playing, or planning the next opportunity to play?

2. Do you need to spend more time and money on video games to feel the same amount of excitement as other activities in your life?

3. Have you tried to play video games for shorter durations of time but have been unsuccessful?

4. Do you become restless or irritable when you attempt to cut down or stop playing video games?

5. Have you played video games as a way to escape problems or negative feelings?

6. Have you lied to family or friends about how much you play video games?

7. Have you ever stolen a video game from a store or a friend or stolen money to buy a video game?

8. Do you sometimes skip household chores in order to play more video games?

9. Do you sometimes skip homework or work in order to play more video games?

10. Have you ever done poorly on a school assignment, test, or work assignment because you spent so much time playing video games?

11. Have you ever needed friends or family to give you extra money because you've spent too much of your own money on video games, software, or internet game fees?

Individuals who respond "yes" to six or more of these questions are most likely struggling with video game addiction.

Made in the USA
Las Vegas, NV
26 February 2021